THE MANGA BIBLE

KJV EDITION 1611

Thanks to Hodder Headline for use of Manga BIble Images and Manga Jesus Images which are wholly owned by Siku.

First published in Great Britain in 2011
by Edge Group,
PO BOX LB 631
Rathbone Place, London W1 1HQ

ISBN: 978-0-956731-1-5

Dedications by Publisher Ed Chatelier and Edge Group

CELEBRATING THE WEDDING of
MARK and HAYLEY CHATELIER on 25-11-2011.

Also celebrating on this special occasion father Trevor, Grandmother Barbara and twin brother Paul Chatelier.

And the Lord God said, it is not good that the man should be alone; I will make him an help meet for him. Genesis 2:18

ALSO in the Year of 2011 KJV Anniversary

IN MEMORY

In Memory of Mike Clinch who passed away 31 August 2011 ex MD of Logitag UK , Manager at BT TELEX and UNIX expert. He leaves his wife Jenny and children Jonathan and Deborah. ' A great family Man and a man of integrity and faith.'

Precious in the HIS sight is the death of his Saints. Psalm 116:15

Dedications by the author

Dedicated to William Tyndale who started it all.
His, was the first English translation to draw directly from the Hebrew and Greek text. He was the first to exploit the new medium of print, and contributed much to the English vocabulary.
He would later suffer imprisonment, choking, impalement and burning for his work.
The King James Version is based on his trailblazing work.

Thank you Lord, for the life of W. Tyndale.
Amen.

PREFACE

I grew up learning to read and understand the King James Version. Her elegant, majestic and authoritative use of the English language had been a companion of mine for over 30 years. Of course, more recent translations are easier to read and understand. Some of the looser translations like the NLT can be surprisingly refreshing and other tighter translations like the NIV and RSV are invaluable tools for serious study. But when I want to recall scripture, I recall her best in the Authorised Version.

When we created *The Manga Bible*, the use of vibrancy and immediacy of the language spoken on the streets was paramount and is largely responsible for the success of that project.
A reissue of parts of *The Manga Bible* with a King James Version seeks to reflect that vibrancy and immediacy as first seen by her English readers in 1611.
It also serves to demonstrate *The Manga Bible's* faithful retelling of the Bible Story.

It would be 400 years since the word of God was made available in native language as God intended. We celebrate this.
The Lord is indeed faithful.

All glory, honour, praise, majesty and love to our King, our Lord Jesus Christ, the Word of God.

Amen.

THE MANGA BIBLE

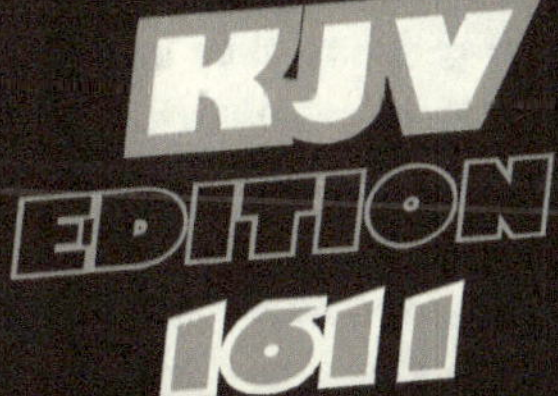

HOW IT ALL STARTED

5 INTERESTING FACTS

FACT: The KJV was commisioned by King James 1 in 1611.
2011 is the 400 hundreth anniversary.

FACT: The KJV was aimed at the common person
so that he/she could read the Word of God firsthand.

HOW IT STARTED- THE KEY MEETING

FACT: The KJV began in 1604 when King James, who succeeded Queen Elizabeth the 1st, called a meeting at Hampton Court in January, 1604, to iron out complaints by the Puritans.

The preface of the Authorized Version states:
... the very historical truth is that upon the importunate petitions of the Puritans, at his Majesty's coming to this crown, the conference at Hampton Court having been appointed for hearing their complaints: when by force of reason they were put from all other grounds, they had recourse at the last, to this shift, that they could not with good conscience subscribe to the Communion [Prayer] book, since it maintained the Bible as it was there translated [in the Great Bible], which was, as they said, a most corrupted translation. And although this was judged to be but a very poor and empty shift, yet even here upon did his Majesty begin to bethink himself of the good that might ensue by a new translation, and presently after gave order for this translation which is now presented unto thee.

FACT: KJV TURNING POINT

The Hampton Court Conference was drifting into sectarian arguments, historians note, when Puritan leader John Rainolds (also spelled Reynolds), took the bold step of addressing James and asking for a new translation of the Bible, since the previous Bibles "were corrupt and not answerable to the truth of the original." KING JAMES was delighted AND SO FROM THIS MEETING stemmed the KJV.

FACT: The King James TEXT has since not been revised. It has only been proof edited to correct typographical errors, add notes, and omit the Apocrypha from between the Testaments.

FACT: The KJV can be read in approximately 70 hours . "I have no greater joy than to hear that my children walk in truth" (III John 4).

FACT: The KJV was regarded as This "translation to end all translations" (for a while at least) was the result of the combined effort of about fifty scholars (later reduced to 47). They utilised : The Tyndale New Testament, The Coverdale Bible, The Matthews Bible, The Great Bible, The Geneva Bible, and even the Rheims New Testament.

The great revision of the Bishop's Bible had begun. From 1605 to 1606 the scholars studied in private research. From 1607 to 1609 the work was constructed. In 1610 the manuscript went to press, and in 1611 the first of the huge (16 inch tall) pulpit bible known today as "The 1611 King James Bible" came off the printing press.

IN THE BEGINNING GOD CREATED THE HEAVEN AND THE EARTH...

GENESIS

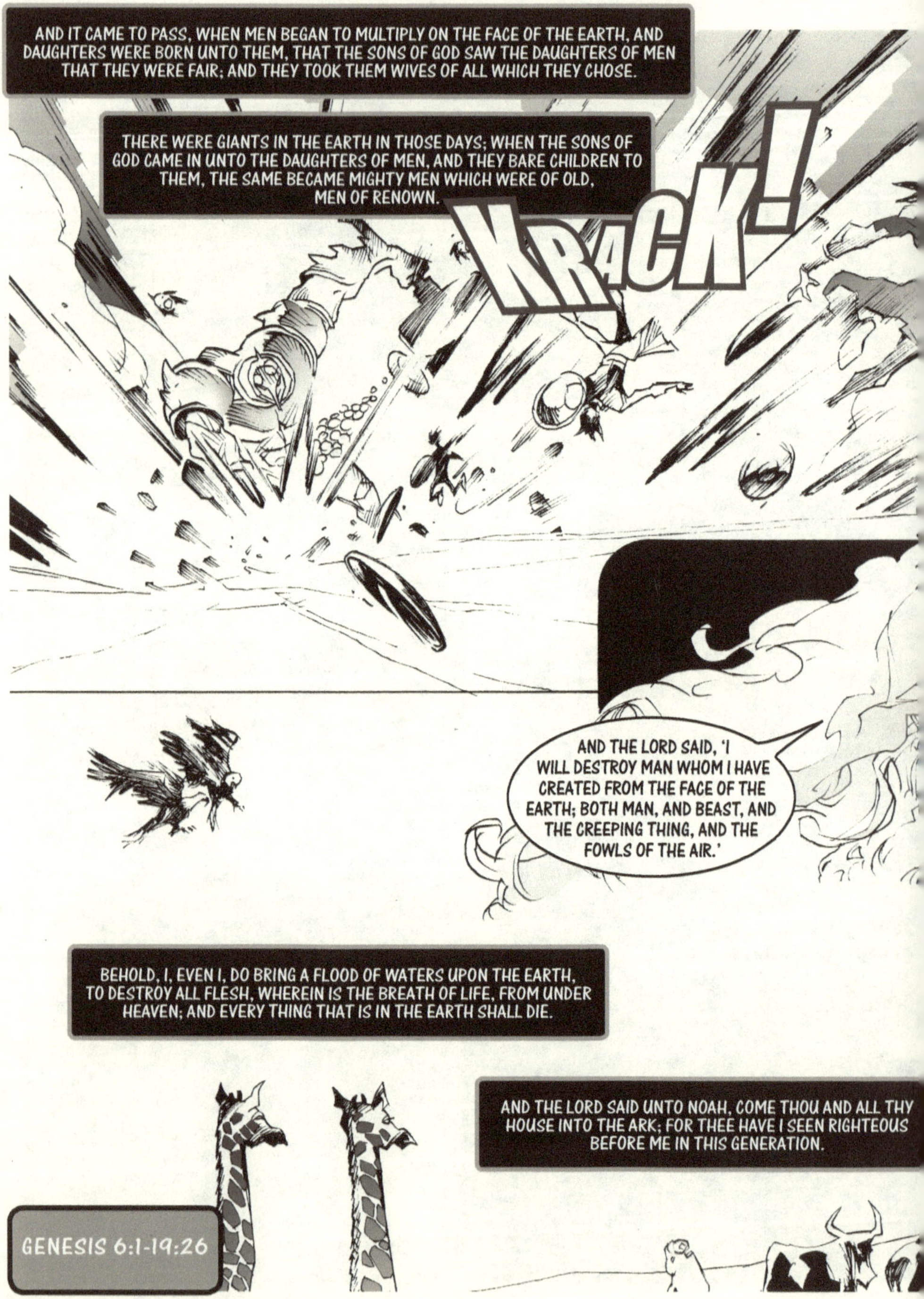

AND IT CAME TO PASS, WHEN MEN BEGAN TO MULTIPLY ON THE FACE OF THE EARTH, AND DAUGHTERS WERE BORN UNTO THEM, THAT THE SONS OF GOD SAW THE DAUGHTERS OF MEN THAT THEY WERE FAIR; AND THEY TOOK THEM WIVES OF ALL WHICH THEY CHOSE.

THERE WERE GIANTS IN THE EARTH IN THOSE DAYS; WHEN THE SONS OF GOD CAME IN UNTO THE DAUGHTERS OF MEN, AND THEY BARE CHILDREN TO THEM, THE SAME BECAME MIGHTY MEN WHICH WERE OF OLD, MEN OF RENOWN.

KRACK!

AND THE LORD SAID, 'I WILL DESTROY MAN WHOM I HAVE CREATED FROM THE FACE OF THE EARTH; BOTH MAN, AND BEAST, AND THE CREEPING THING, AND THE FOWLS OF THE AIR.'

BEHOLD, I, EVEN I, DO BRING A FLOOD OF WATERS UPON THE EARTH, TO DESTROY ALL FLESH, WHEREIN IS THE BREATH OF LIFE, FROM UNDER HEAVEN; AND EVERY THING THAT IS IN THE EARTH SHALL DIE.

AND THE LORD SAID UNTO NOAH, COME THOU AND ALL THY HOUSE INTO THE ARK; FOR THEE HAVE I SEEN RIGHTEOUS BEFORE ME IN THIS GENERATION.

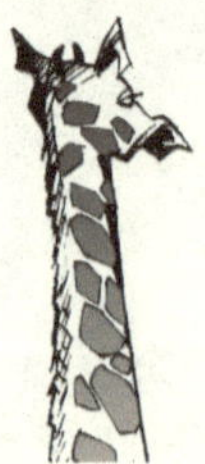

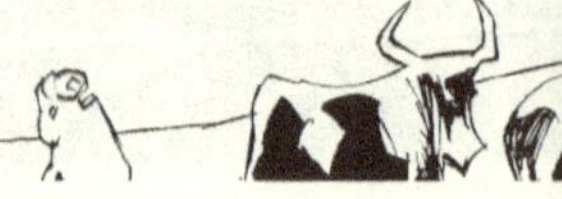

GENESIS 6:1-19:26

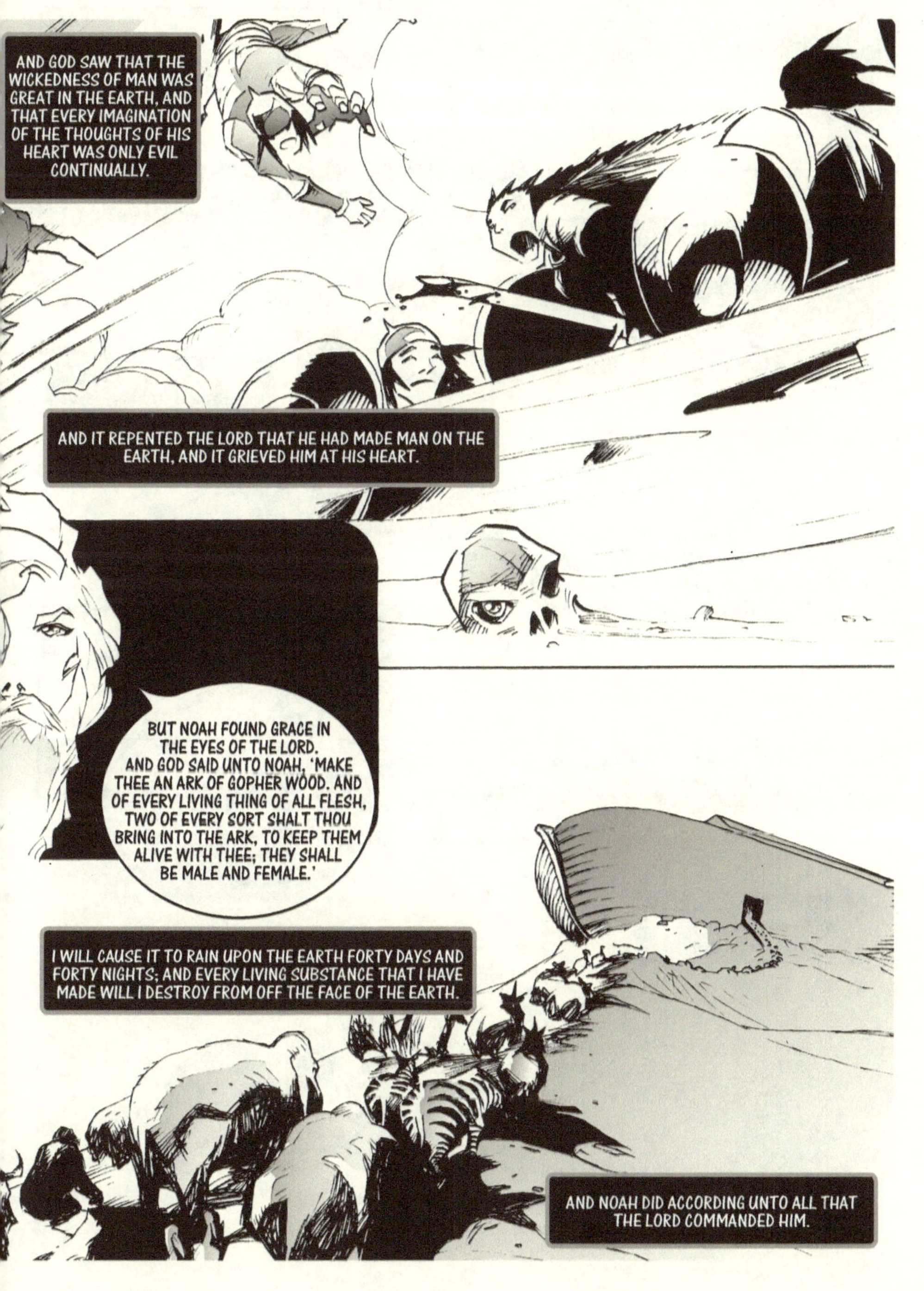
AND GOD SAW THAT THE WICKEDNESS OF MAN WAS GREAT IN THE EARTH, AND THAT EVERY IMAGINATION OF THE THOUGHTS OF HIS HEART WAS ONLY EVIL CONTINUALLY.
AND IT REPENTED THE LORD THAT HE HAD MADE MAN ON THE EARTH, AND IT GRIEVED HIM AT HIS HEART.
BUT NOAH FOUND GRACE IN THE EYES OF THE LORD. AND GOD SAID UNTO NOAH, 'MAKE THEE AN ARK OF GOPHER WOOD. AND OF EVERY LIVING THING OF ALL FLESH, TWO OF EVERY SORT SHALT THOU BRING INTO THE ARK, TO KEEP THEM ALIVE WITH THEE; THEY SHALL BE MALE AND FEMALE.'
I WILL CAUSE IT TO RAIN UPON THE EARTH FORTY DAYS AND FORTY NIGHTS; AND EVERY LIVING SUBSTANCE THAT I HAVE MADE WILL I DESTROY FROM OFF THE FACE OF THE EARTH.
AND NOAH DID ACCORDING UNTO ALL THAT THE LORD COMMANDED HIM.

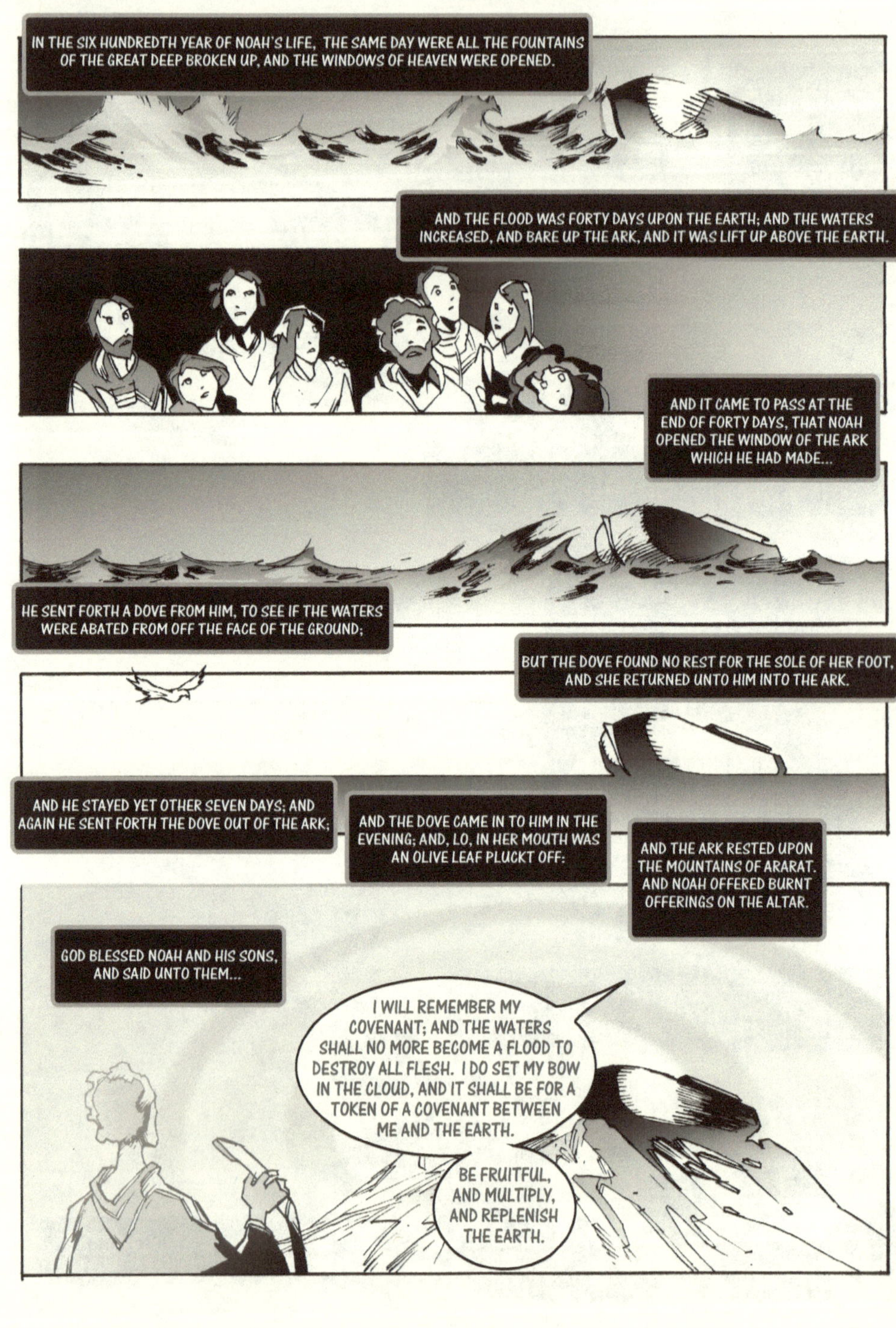
IN THE SIX HUNDREDTH YEAR OF NOAH'S LIFE, THE SAME DAY WERE ALL THE FOUNTAINS OF THE GREAT DEEP BROKEN UP, AND THE WINDOWS OF HEAVEN WERE OPENED.
AND THE FLOOD WAS FORTY DAYS UPON THE EARTH; AND THE WATERS INCREASED, AND BARE UP THE ARK, AND IT WAS LIFT UP ABOVE THE EARTH.
AND IT CAME TO PASS AT THE END OF FORTY DAYS, THAT NOAH OPENED THE WINDOW OF THE ARK WHICH HE HAD MADE...
HE SENT FORTH A DOVE FROM HIM, TO SEE IF THE WATERS WERE ABATED FROM OFF THE FACE OF THE GROUND;
BUT THE DOVE FOUND NO REST FOR THE SOLE OF HER FOOT, AND SHE RETURNED UNTO HIM INTO THE ARK.
AND HE STAYED YET OTHER SEVEN DAYS; AND AGAIN HE SENT FORTH THE DOVE OUT OF THE ARK;
AND THE DOVE CAME IN TO HIM IN THE EVENING; AND, LO, IN HER MOUTH WAS AN OLIVE LEAF PLUCKT OFF:
AND THE ARK RESTED UPON THE MOUNTAINS OF ARARAT. AND NOAH OFFERED BURNT OFFERINGS ON THE ALTAR.
GOD BLESSED NOAH AND HIS SONS, AND SAID UNTO THEM...
I WILL REMEMBER MY COVENANT; AND THE WATERS SHALL NO MORE BECOME A FLOOD TO DESTROY ALL FLESH. I DO SET MY BOW IN THE CLOUD, AND IT SHALL BE FOR A TOKEN OF A COVENANT BETWEEN ME AND THE EARTH.
BE FRUITFUL, AND MULTIPLY, AND REPLENISH THE EARTH.

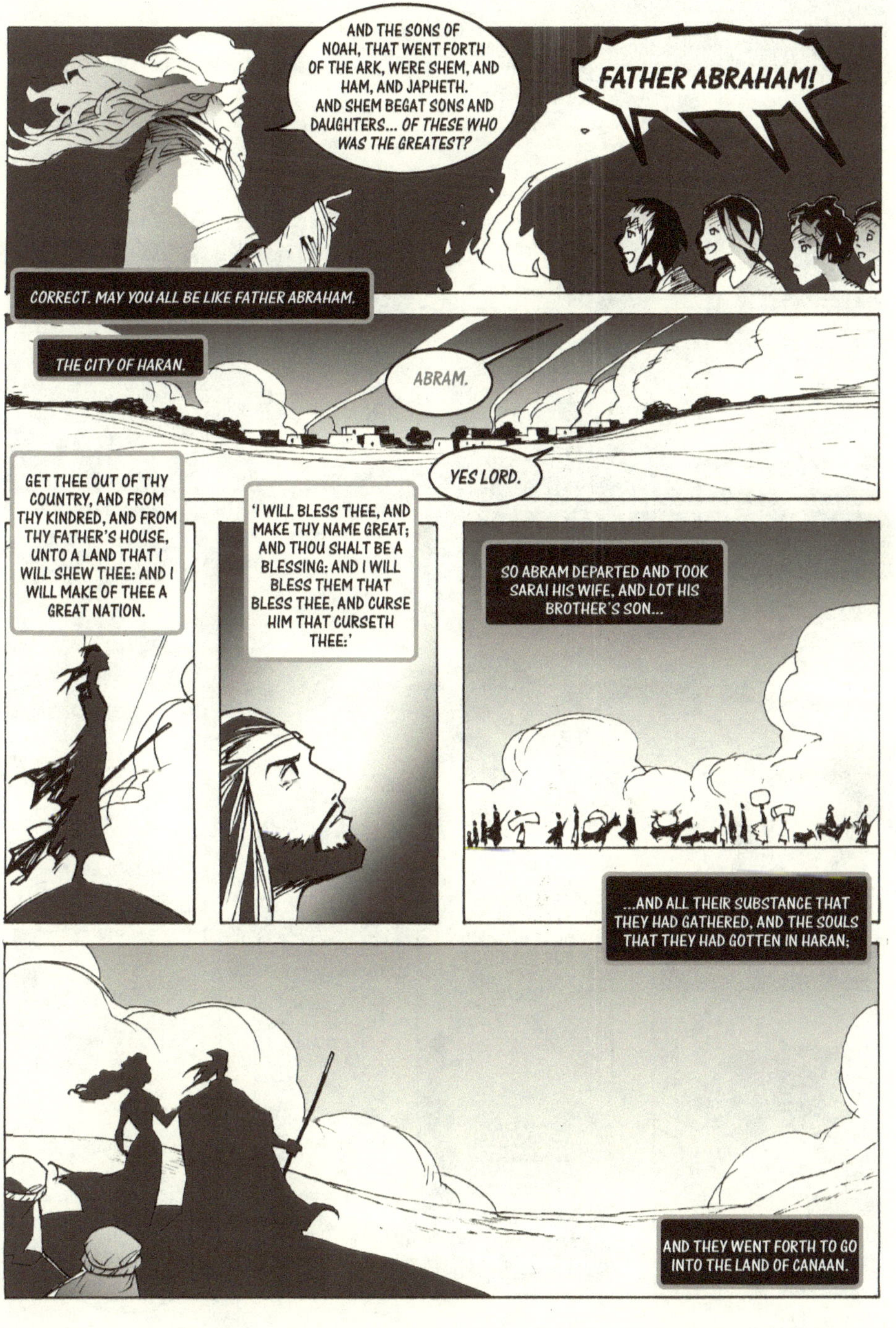
AND THE SONS OF NOAH, THAT WENT FORTH OF THE ARK, WERE SHEM, AND HAM, AND JAPHETH. AND SHEM BEGAT SONS AND DAUGHTERS... OF THESE WHO WAS THE GREATEST?
FATHER ABRAHAM!
CORRECT. MAY YOU ALL BE LIKE FATHER ABRAHAM.
THE CITY OF HARAN.
ABRAM.
YES LORD.
GET THEE OUT OF THY COUNTRY, AND FROM THY KINDRED, AND FROM THY FATHER'S HOUSE, UNTO A LAND THAT I WILL SHEW THEE: AND I WILL MAKE OF THEE A GREAT NATION.
'I WILL BLESS THEE, AND MAKE THY NAME GREAT; AND THOU SHALT BE A BLESSING: AND I WILL BLESS THEM THAT BLESS THEE, AND CURSE HIM THAT CURSETH THEE:'
SO ABRAM DEPARTED AND TOOK SARAI HIS WIFE, AND LOT HIS BROTHER'S SON...
...AND ALL THEIR SUBSTANCE THAT THEY HAD GATHERED, AND THE SOULS THAT THEY HAD GOTTEN IN HARAN;
AND THEY WENT FORTH TO GO INTO THE LAND OF CANAAN.

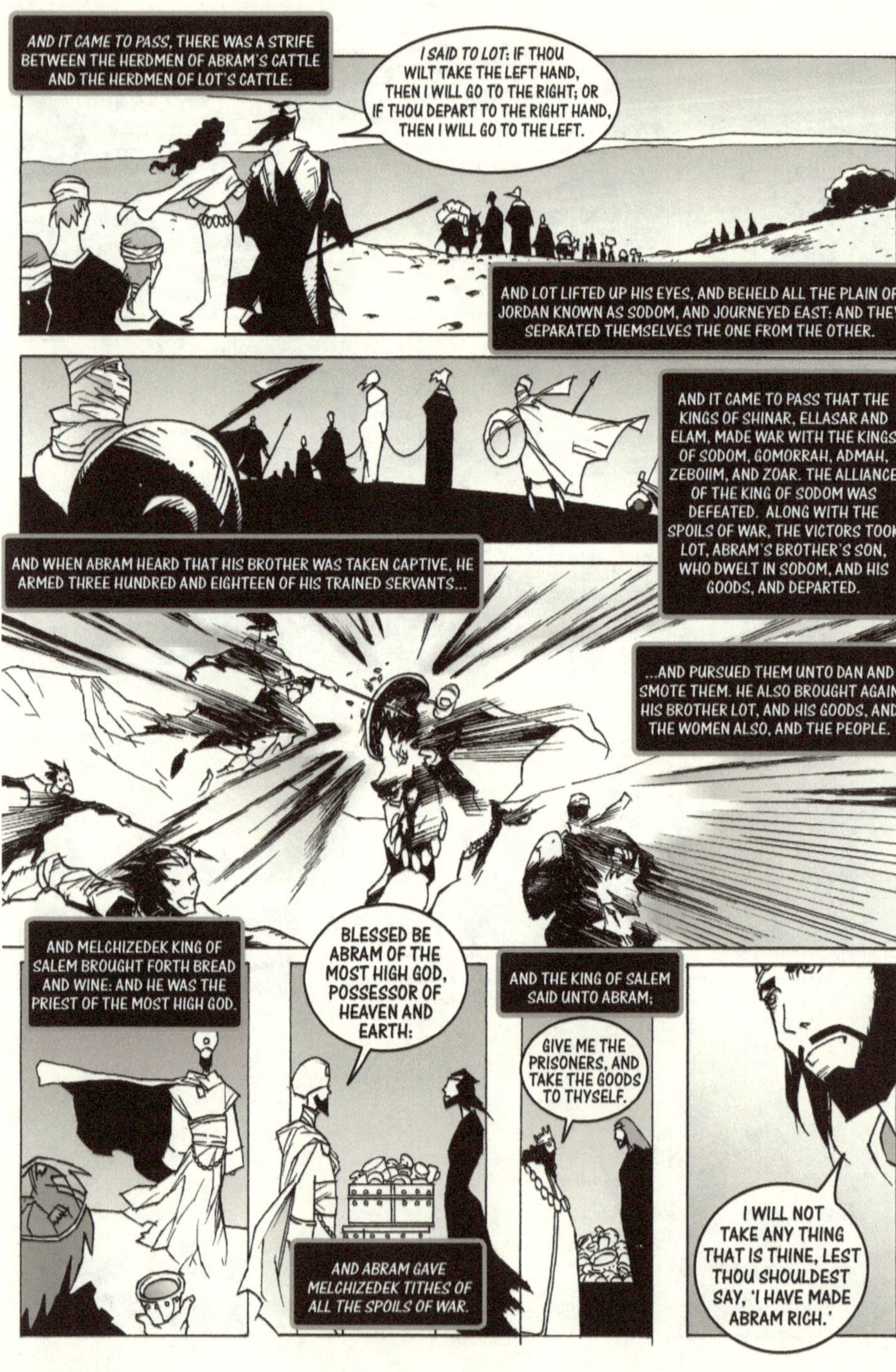
AND IT CAME TO PASS, THERE WAS A STRIFE BETWEEN THE HERDMEN OF ABRAM'S CATTLE AND THE HERDMEN OF LOT'S CATTLE:
I SAID TO LOT: IF THOU WILT TAKE THE LEFT HAND, THEN I WILL GO TO THE RIGHT; OR IF THOU DEPART TO THE RIGHT HAND, THEN I WILL GO TO THE LEFT.
AND LOT LIFTED UP HIS EYES, AND BEHELD ALL THE PLAIN OF JORDAN KNOWN AS SODOM, AND JOURNEYED EAST: AND THEY SEPARATED THEMSELVES THE ONE FROM THE OTHER.
AND IT CAME TO PASS THAT THE KINGS OF SHINAR, ELLASAR AND ELAM, MADE WAR WITH THE KINGS OF SODOM, GOMORRAH, ADMAH, ZEBOIIM, AND ZOAR. THE ALLIANCE OF THE KING OF SODOM WAS DEFEATED. ALONG WITH THE SPOILS OF WAR, THE VICTORS TOOK LOT, ABRAM'S BROTHER'S SON, WHO DWELT IN SODOM, AND HIS GOODS, AND DEPARTED.
AND WHEN ABRAM HEARD THAT HIS BROTHER WAS TAKEN CAPTIVE, HE ARMED THREE HUNDRED AND EIGHTEEN OF HIS TRAINED SERVANTS...
...AND PURSUED THEM UNTO DAN AND SMOTE THEM. HE ALSO BROUGHT AGAIN HIS BROTHER LOT, AND HIS GOODS, AND THE WOMEN ALSO, AND THE PEOPLE.
AND MELCHIZEDEK KING OF SALEM BROUGHT FORTH BREAD AND WINE: AND HE WAS THE PRIEST OF THE MOST HIGH GOD.
BLESSED BE ABRAM OF THE MOST HIGH GOD, POSSESSOR OF HEAVEN AND EARTH:
AND ABRAM GAVE MELCHIZEDEK TITHES OF ALL THE SPOILS OF WAR.
AND THE KING OF SALEM SAID UNTO ABRAM;
GIVE ME THE PRISONERS, AND TAKE THE GOODS TO THYSELF.
I WILL NOT TAKE ANY THING THAT IS THINE, LEST THOU SHOULDEST SAY, 'I HAVE MADE ABRAM RICH.'

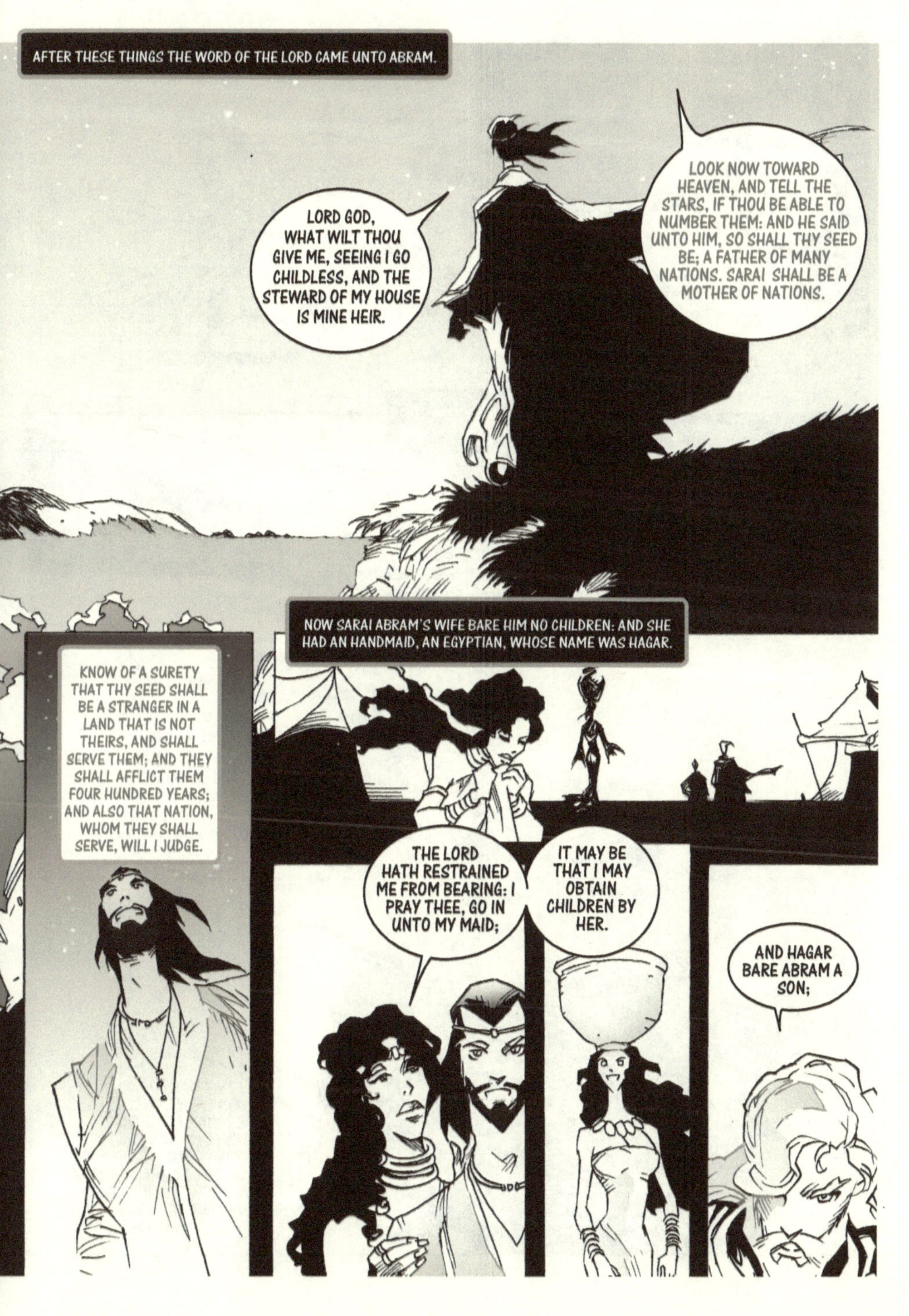
AFTER THESE THINGS THE WORD OF THE LORD CAME UNTO ABRAM.
LORD GOD, WHAT WILT THOU GIVE ME, SEEING I GO CHILDLESS, AND THE STEWARD OF MY HOUSE IS MINE HEIR.
LOOK NOW TOWARD HEAVEN, AND TELL THE STARS, IF THOU BE ABLE TO NUMBER THEM: AND HE SAID UNTO HIM, SO SHALL THY SEED BE; A FATHER OF MANY NATIONS. SARAI SHALL BE A MOTHER OF NATIONS.
KNOW OF A SURETY THAT THY SEED SHALL BE A STRANGER IN A LAND THAT IS NOT THEIRS, AND SHALL SERVE THEM; AND THEY SHALL AFFLICT THEM FOUR HUNDRED YEARS; AND ALSO THAT NATION, WHOM THEY SHALL SERVE, WILL I JUDGE.
NOW SARAI ABRAM'S WIFE BARE HIM NO CHILDREN: AND SHE HAD AN HANDMAID, AN EGYPTIAN, WHOSE NAME WAS HAGAR.
THE LORD HATH RESTRAINED ME FROM BEARING: I PRAY THEE, GO IN UNTO MY MAID;
IT MAY BE THAT I MAY OBTAIN CHILDREN BY HER.
AND HAGAR BARE ABRAM A SON;

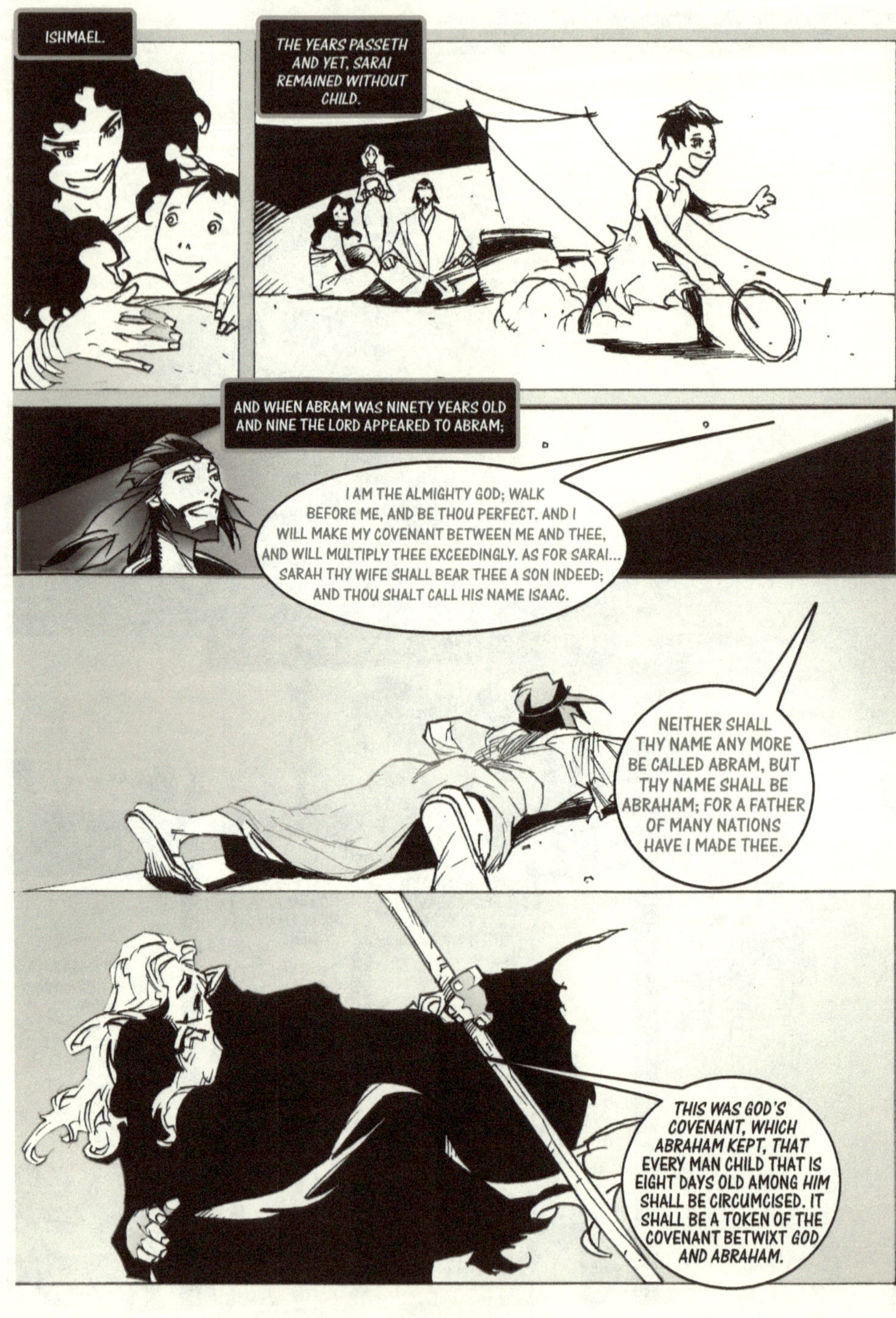

ISHMAEL.
THE YEARS PASSETH AND YET, SARAI REMAINED WITHOUT CHILD.
AND WHEN ABRAM WAS NINETY YEARS OLD AND NINE THE LORD APPEARED TO ABRAM;
I AM THE ALMIGHTY GOD; WALK BEFORE ME, AND BE THOU PERFECT. AND I WILL MAKE MY COVENANT BETWEEN ME AND THEE, AND WILL MULTIPLY THEE EXCEEDINGLY. AS FOR SARAI... SARAH THY WIFE SHALL BEAR THEE A SON INDEED; AND THOU SHALT CALL HIS NAME ISAAC.
NEITHER SHALL THY NAME ANY MORE BE CALLED ABRAM, BUT THY NAME SHALL BE ABRAHAM; FOR A FATHER OF MANY NATIONS HAVE I MADE THEE.
THIS WAS GOD'S COVENANT, WHICH ABRAHAM KEPT, THAT EVERY MAN CHILD THAT IS EIGHT DAYS OLD AMONG *HIM* SHALL BE CIRCUMCISED. IT SHALL BE A TOKEN OF THE COVENANT BETWIXT *GOD* AND ABRAHAM.

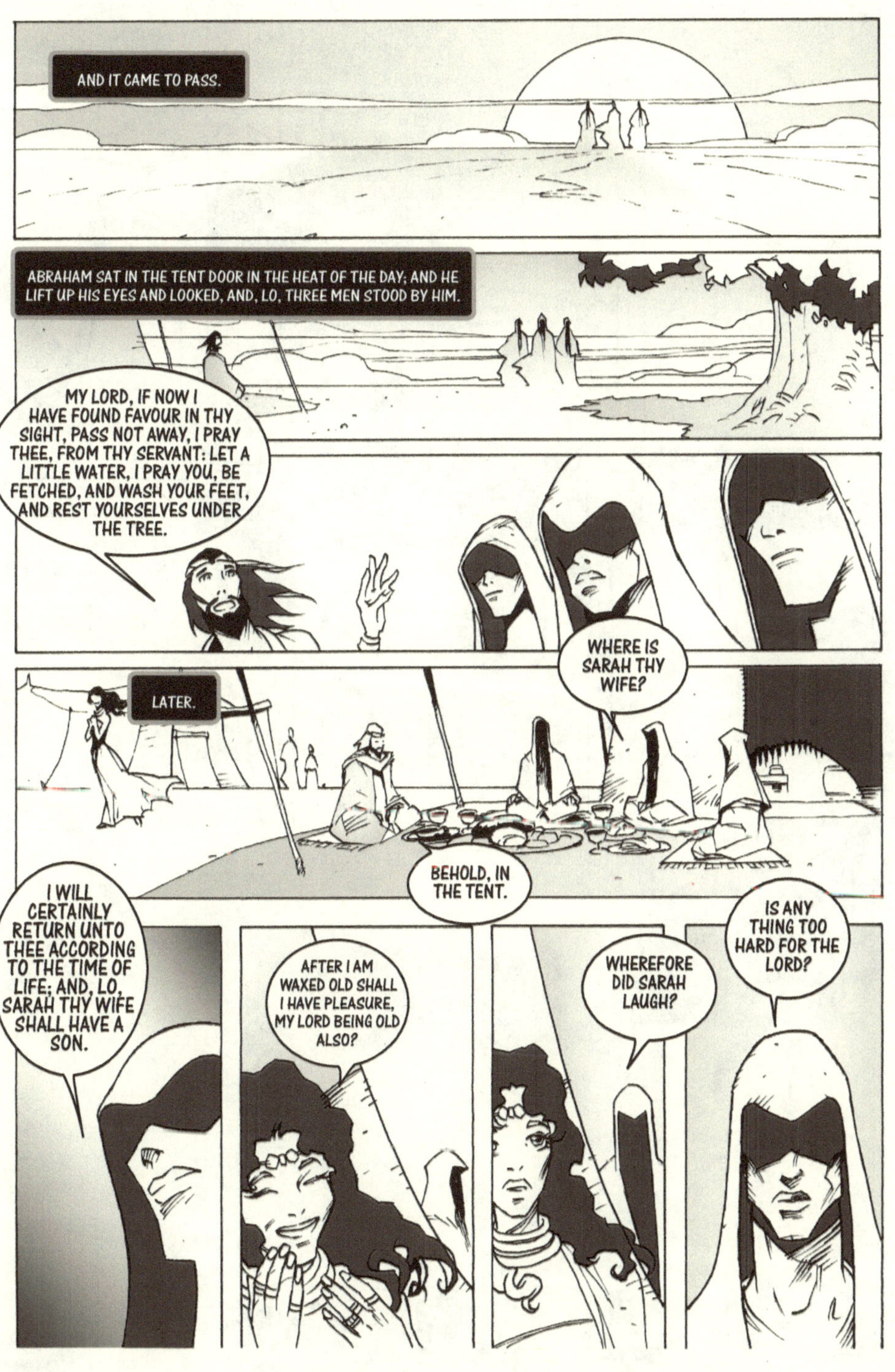

AND IT CAME TO PASS.
ABRAHAM SAT IN THE TENT DOOR IN THE HEAT OF THE DAY; AND HE LIFT UP HIS EYES AND LOOKED, AND, LO, THREE MEN STOOD BY HIM.
MY LORD, IF NOW I HAVE FOUND FAVOUR IN THY SIGHT, PASS NOT AWAY, I PRAY THEE, FROM THY SERVANT: LET A LITTLE WATER, I PRAY YOU, BE FETCHED, AND WASH YOUR FEET, AND REST YOURSELVES UNDER THE TREE.
LATER.
WHERE IS SARAH THY WIFE?
BEHOLD, IN THE TENT.
I WILL CERTAINLY RETURN UNTO THEE ACCORDING TO THE TIME OF LIFE; AND, LO, SARAH THY WIFE SHALL HAVE A SON.
AFTER I AM WAXED OLD SHALL I HAVE PLEASURE, MY LORD BEING OLD ALSO?
WHEREFORE DID SARAH LAUGH?
IS ANY THING TOO HARD FOR THE LORD?

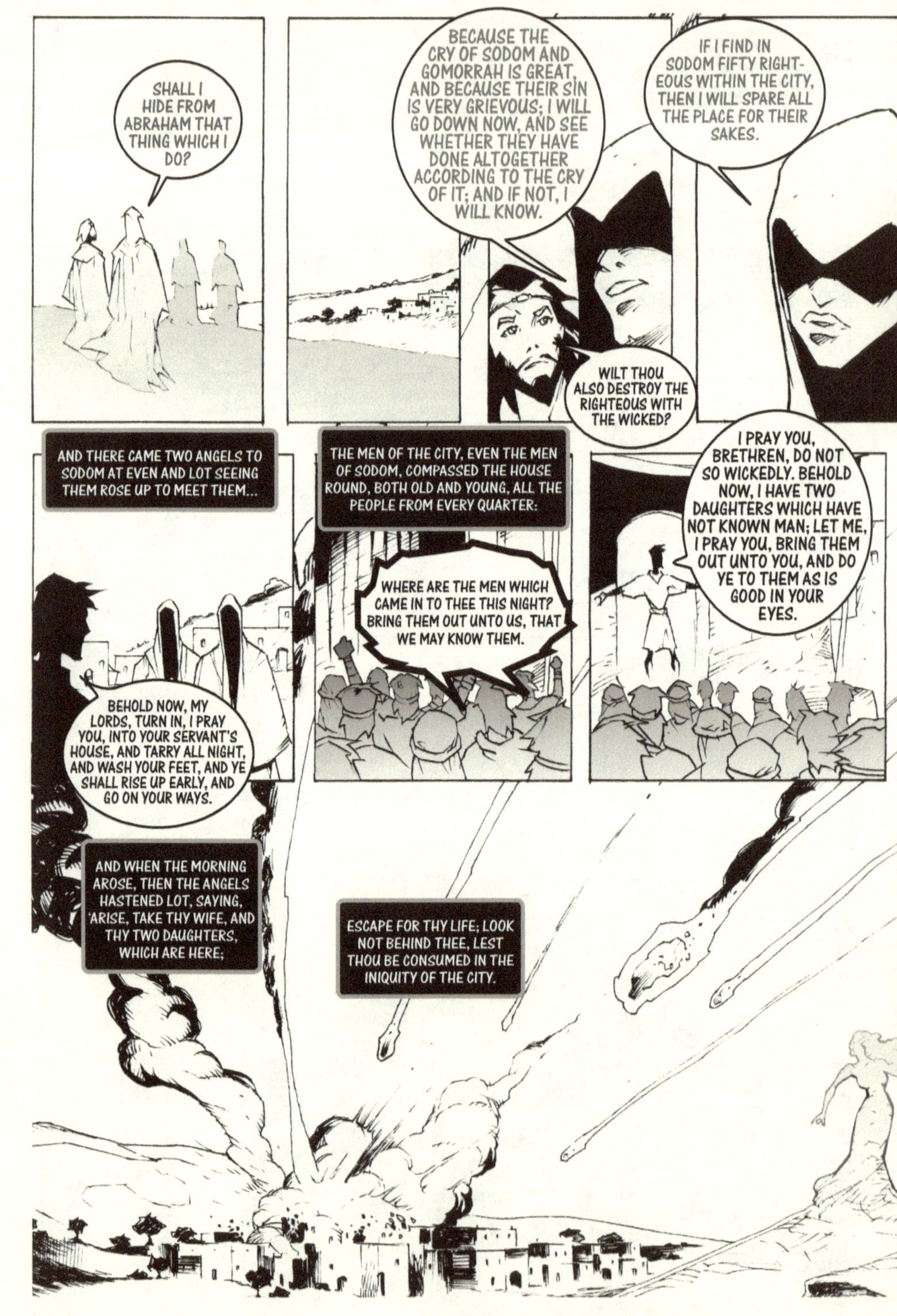
SHALL I HIDE FROM ABRAHAM THAT THING WHICH I DO?
BECAUSE THE CRY OF SODOM AND GOMORRAH IS GREAT, AND BECAUSE THEIR SIN IS VERY GRIEVOUS; I WILL GO DOWN NOW, AND SEE WHETHER THEY HAVE DONE ALTOGETHER ACCORDING TO THE CRY OF IT; AND IF NOT, I WILL KNOW.
WILT THOU ALSO DESTROY THE RIGHTEOUS WITH THE WICKED?
IF I FIND IN SODOM FIFTY RIGHT-EOUS WITHIN THE CITY, THEN I WILL SPARE ALL THE PLACE FOR THEIR SAKES.
AND THERE CAME TWO ANGELS TO SODOM AT EVEN AND LOT SEEING THEM ROSE UP TO MEET THEM...
BEHOLD NOW, MY LORDS, TURN IN, I PRAY YOU, INTO YOUR SERVANT'S HOUSE, AND TARRY ALL NIGHT, AND WASH YOUR FEET, AND YE SHALL RISE UP EARLY, AND GO ON YOUR WAYS.
THE MEN OF THE CITY, EVEN THE MEN OF SODOM, COMPASSED THE HOUSE ROUND, BOTH OLD AND YOUNG, ALL THE PEOPLE FROM EVERY QUARTER:
WHERE ARE THE MEN WHICH CAME IN TO THEE THIS NIGHT? BRING THEM OUT UNTO US, THAT WE MAY KNOW THEM.
I PRAY YOU, BRETHREN, DO NOT SO WICKEDLY. BEHOLD NOW, I HAVE TWO DAUGHTERS WHICH HAVE NOT KNOWN MAN; LET ME, I PRAY YOU, BRING THEM OUT UNTO YOU, AND DO YE TO THEM AS IS GOOD IN YOUR EYES.
AND WHEN THE MORNING AROSE, THEN THE ANGELS HASTENED LOT, SAYING, 'ARISE, TAKE THY WIFE, AND THY TWO DAUGHTERS, WHICH ARE HERE;
ESCAPE FOR THY LIFE; LOOK NOT BEHIND THEE, LEST THOU BE CONSUMED IN THE INIQUITY OF THE CITY.

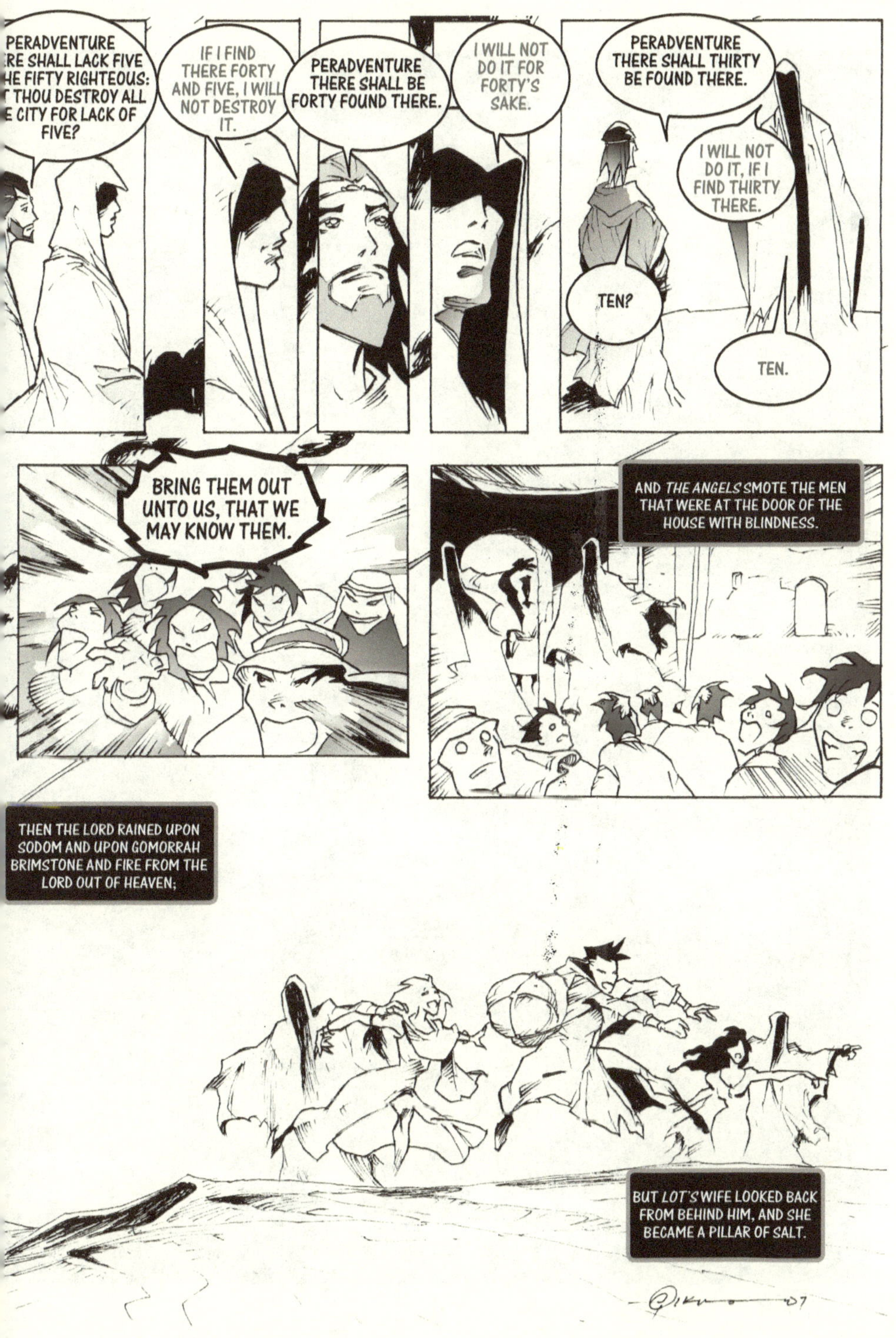

PERADVENTURE ERE SHALL LACK FIVE HE FIFTY RIGHTEOUS: T THOU DESTROY ALL E CITY FOR LACK OF FIVE?
IF I FIND THERE FORTY AND FIVE, I WILL NOT DESTROY IT.
PERADVENTURE THERE SHALL BE FORTY FOUND THERE.
I WILL NOT DO IT FOR FORTY'S SAKE.
PERADVENTURE THERE SHALL THIRTY BE FOUND THERE.
I WILL NOT DO IT, IF I FIND THIRTY THERE.
TEN?
TEN.
BRING THEM OUT UNTO US, THAT WE MAY KNOW THEM.
AND THE ANGELS SMOTE THE MEN THAT WERE AT THE DOOR OF THE HOUSE WITH BLINDNESS.
THEN THE LORD RAINED UPON SODOM AND UPON GOMORRAH BRIMSTONE AND FIRE FROM THE LORD OUT OF HEAVEN;
BUT LOT'S WIFE LOOKED BACK FROM BEHIND HIM, AND SHE BECAME A PILLAR OF SALT.

IN THE BEGINNING GOD
CREATED THE HEAVEN AND THE
EARTH...

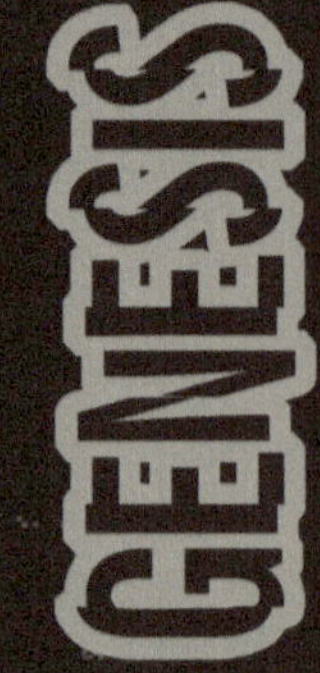

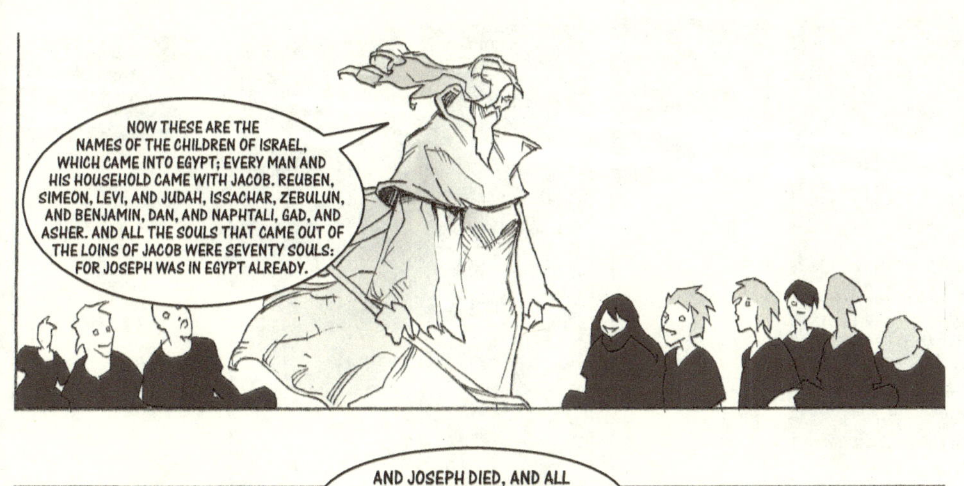

AND JOSEPH DIED, AND ALL HIS BRETHREN, AND ALL THAT GENERATION.

AND THE CHILDREN OF ISRAEL WERE FRUITFUL, AND INCREASED ABUNDANTLY, AND MULTIPLIED, AND WAXED EXCEEDING MIGHTY; AND THE LAND WAS FILLED WITH THEM. NOW THERE AROSE UP A NEW KING OVER EGYPT, WHICH KNEW NOT JOSEPH.

AND HE SAID UNTO HIS PEOPLE,...

BEHOLD, THE PEOPLE OF THE CHILDREN OF ISRAEL ARE MORE AND MIGHTIER THAN WE:

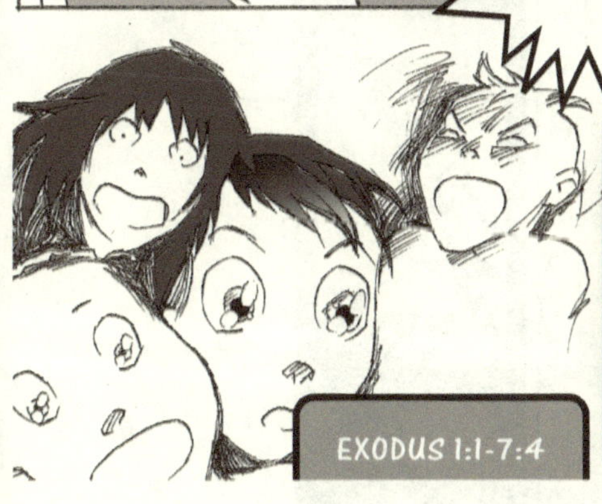

EXODUS 1:1-7:4

AND THE EGYPTIANS MADE THE CHILDREN OF ISRAEL TO SERVE WITH RIGOUR: AND THEY MADE THEIR LIVES BITTER WITH HARD BONDAGE, IN MORTER, AND IN BRICK, AND IN ALL MANNER OF SERVICE IN THE FIELD:... AND PHARAOH CHARGED ALL HIS PEOPLE, SAYING, EVERY SON THAT IS BORN YE SHALL CAST INTO THE RIVER, AND EVERY DAUGHTER YE SHALL SAVE ALIVE.

BUT THE MIDWIVES FEARED GOD, AND DID NOT AS THE KING OF EGYPT COMMANDED THEM, BUT SAVED THE MEN CHILDREN ALIVE.

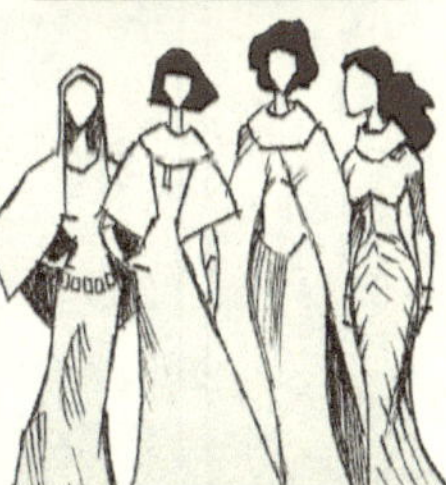

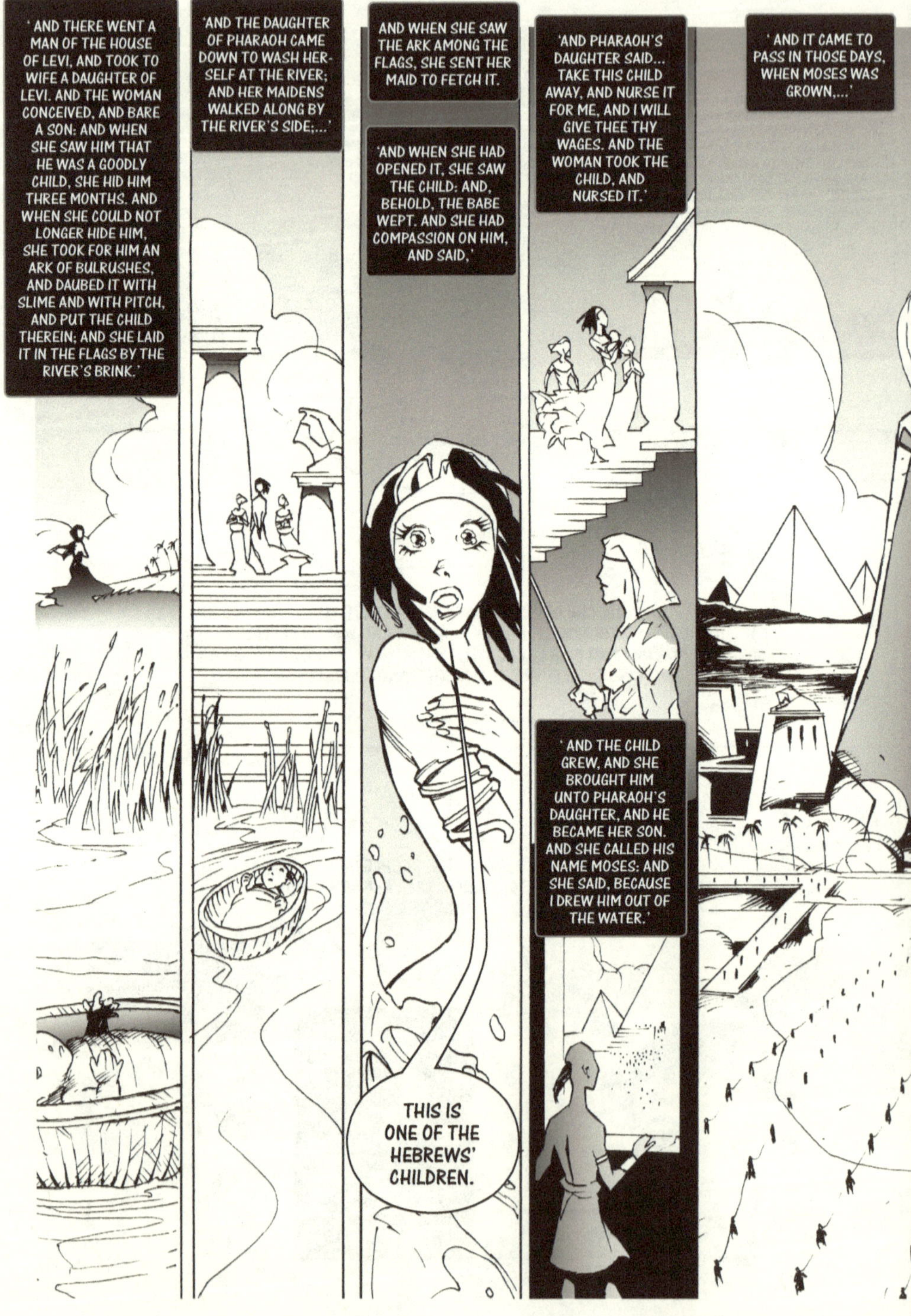
' AND THERE WENT A MAN OF THE HOUSE OF LEVI, AND TOOK TO WIFE A DAUGHTER OF LEVI. AND THE WOMAN CONCEIVED, AND BARE A SON: AND WHEN SHE SAW HIM THAT HE WAS A GOODLY CHILD, SHE HID HIM THREE MONTHS. AND WHEN SHE COULD NOT LONGER HIDE HIM, SHE TOOK FOR HIM AN ARK OF BULRUSHES, AND DAUBED IT WITH SLIME AND WITH PITCH, AND PUT THE CHILD THEREIN; AND SHE LAID IT IN THE FLAGS BY THE RIVER'S BRINK.'
'AND THE DAUGHTER OF PHARAOH CAME DOWN TO WASH HER-SELF AT THE RIVER; AND HER MAIDENS WALKED ALONG BY THE RIVER'S SIDE;...'
AND WHEN SHE SAW THE ARK AMONG THE FLAGS, SHE SENT HER MAID TO FETCH IT.
'AND WHEN SHE HAD OPENED IT, SHE SAW THE CHILD: AND, BEHOLD, THE BABE WEPT. AND SHE HAD COMPASSION ON HIM, AND SAID,'
THIS IS ONE OF THE HEBREWS' CHILDREN.
'AND PHARAOH'S DAUGHTER SAID... TAKE THIS CHILD AWAY, AND NURSE IT FOR ME, AND I WILL GIVE THEE THY WAGES. AND THE WOMAN TOOK THE CHILD, AND NURSED IT.'
' AND THE CHILD GREW, AND SHE BROUGHT HIM UNTO PHARAOH'S DAUGHTER, AND HE BECAME HER SON. AND SHE CALLED HIS NAME MOSES: AND SHE SAID, BECAUSE I DREW HIM OUT OF THE WATER.'
' AND IT CAME TO PASS IN THOSE DAYS, WHEN MOSES WAS GROWN,...'

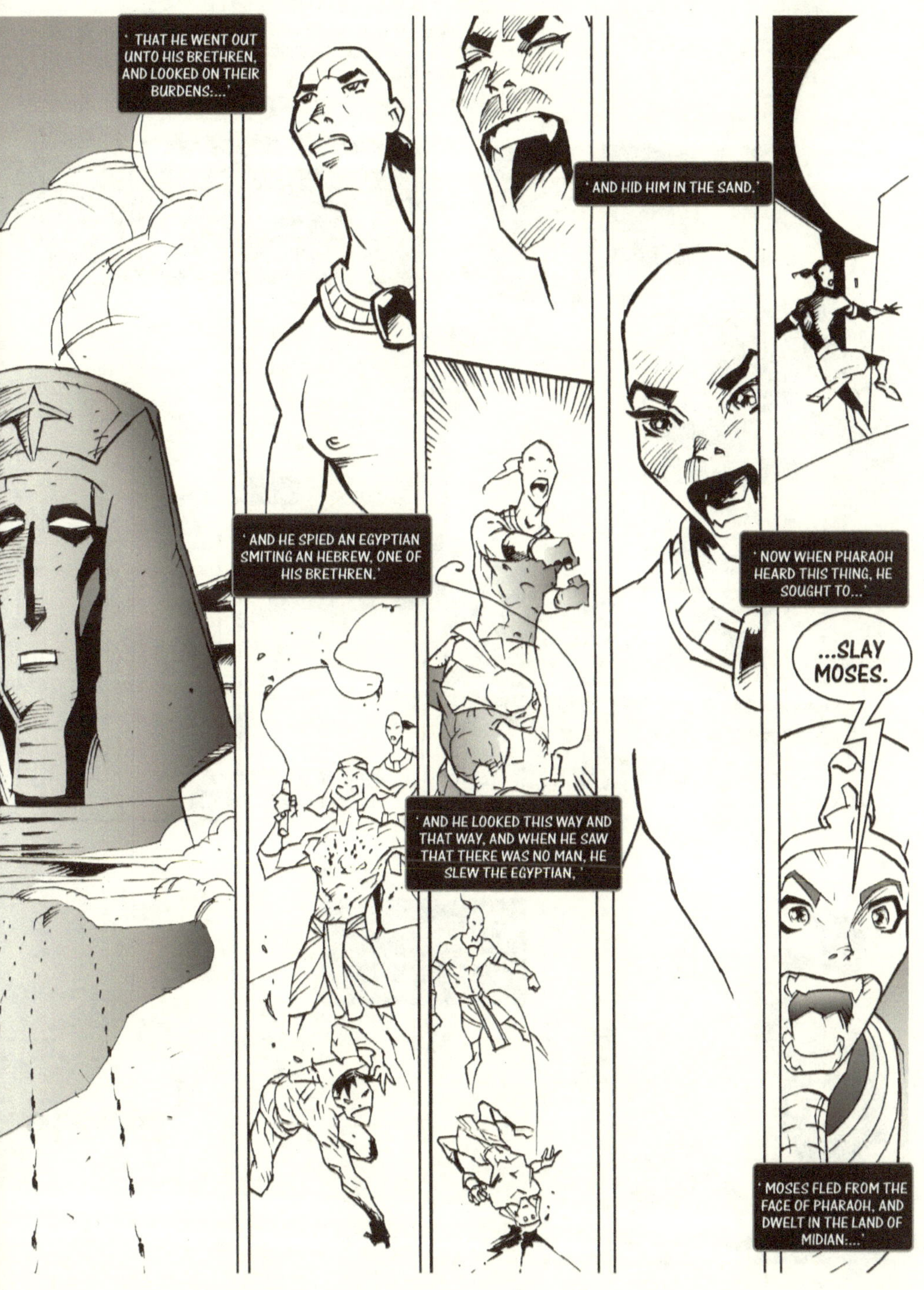
' THAT HE WENT OUT UNTO HIS BRETHREN, AND LOOKED ON THEIR BURDENS:...'
' AND HE SPIED AN EGYPTIAN SMITING AN HEBREW, ONE OF HIS BRETHREN.'
' AND HE LOOKED THIS WAY AND THAT WAY, AND WHEN HE SAW THAT THERE WAS NO MAN, HE SLEW THE EGYPTIAN, '
' AND HID HIM IN THE SAND.'
' NOW WHEN PHARAOH HEARD THIS THING, HE SOUGHT TO...'
...SLAY MOSES.
' MOSES FLED FROM THE FACE OF PHARAOH, AND DWELT IN THE LAND OF MIDIAN:...'

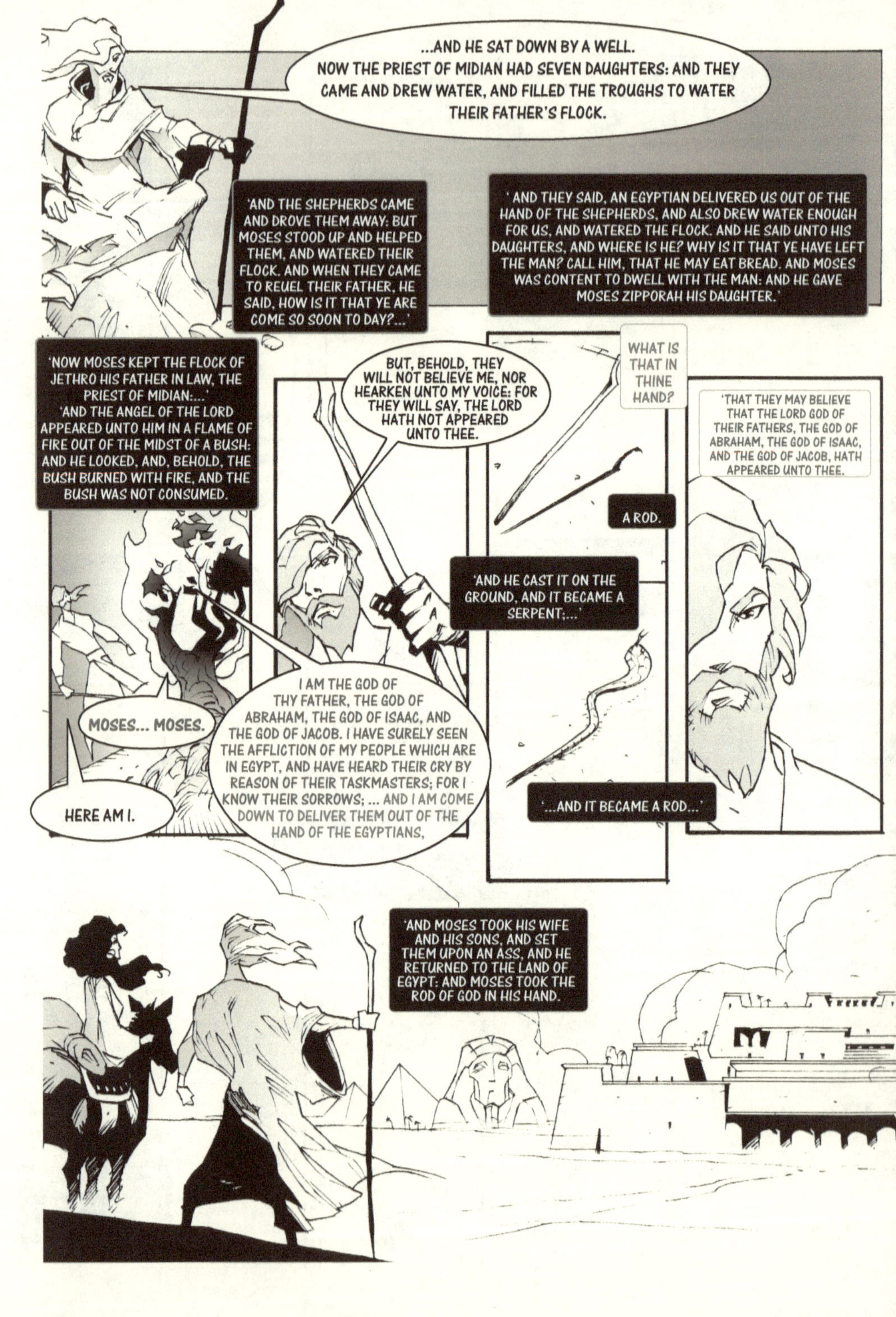
...AND HE SAT DOWN BY A WELL.
NOW THE PRIEST OF MIDIAN HAD SEVEN DAUGHTERS: AND THEY CAME AND DREW WATER, AND FILLED THE TROUGHS TO WATER THEIR FATHER'S FLOCK.
'AND THE SHEPHERDS CAME AND DROVE THEM AWAY: BUT MOSES STOOD UP AND HELPED THEM, AND WATERED THEIR FLOCK. AND WHEN THEY CAME TO REUEL THEIR FATHER, HE SAID, HOW IS IT THAT YE ARE COME SO SOON TO DAY?...'
' AND THEY SAID, AN EGYPTIAN DELIVERED US OUT OF THE HAND OF THE SHEPHERDS, AND ALSO DREW WATER ENOUGH FOR US, AND WATERED THE FLOCK. AND HE SAID UNTO HIS DAUGHTERS, AND WHERE IS HE? WHY IS IT THAT YE HAVE LEFT THE MAN? CALL HIM, THAT HE MAY EAT BREAD. AND MOSES WAS CONTENT TO DWELL WITH THE MAN: AND HE GAVE MOSES ZIPPORAH HIS DAUGHTER.'
'NOW MOSES KEPT THE FLOCK OF JETHRO HIS FATHER IN LAW, THE PRIEST OF MIDIAN:...'
'AND THE ANGEL OF THE LORD APPEARED UNTO HIM IN A FLAME OF FIRE OUT OF THE MIDST OF A BUSH: AND HE LOOKED, AND, BEHOLD, THE BUSH BURNED WITH FIRE, AND THE BUSH WAS NOT CONSUMED.
MOSES... MOSES.
HERE AM I.
I AM THE GOD OF THY FATHER, THE GOD OF ABRAHAM, THE GOD OF ISAAC, AND THE GOD OF JACOB. I HAVE SURELY SEEN THE AFFLICTION OF MY PEOPLE WHICH ARE IN EGYPT, AND HAVE HEARD THEIR CRY BY REASON OF THEIR TASKMASTERS; FOR I KNOW THEIR SORROWS; ... AND I AM COME DOWN TO DELIVER THEM OUT OF THE HAND OF THE EGYPTIANS,
BUT, BEHOLD, THEY WILL NOT BELIEVE ME, NOR HEARKEN UNTO MY VOICE: FOR THEY WILL SAY, THE LORD HATH NOT APPEARED UNTO THEE.
WHAT IS THAT IN THINE HAND?
A ROD.
'AND HE CAST IT ON THE GROUND, AND IT BECAME A SERPENT;...'
'...AND IT BECAME A ROD...'
'THAT THEY MAY BELIEVE THAT THE LORD GOD OF THEIR FATHERS, THE GOD OF ABRAHAM, THE GOD OF ISAAC, AND THE GOD OF JACOB, HATH APPEARED UNTO THEE.
'AND MOSES TOOK HIS WIFE AND HIS SONS, AND SET THEM UPON AN ASS, AND HE RETURNED TO THE LAND OF EGYPT: AND MOSES TOOK THE ROD OF GOD IN HIS HAND.

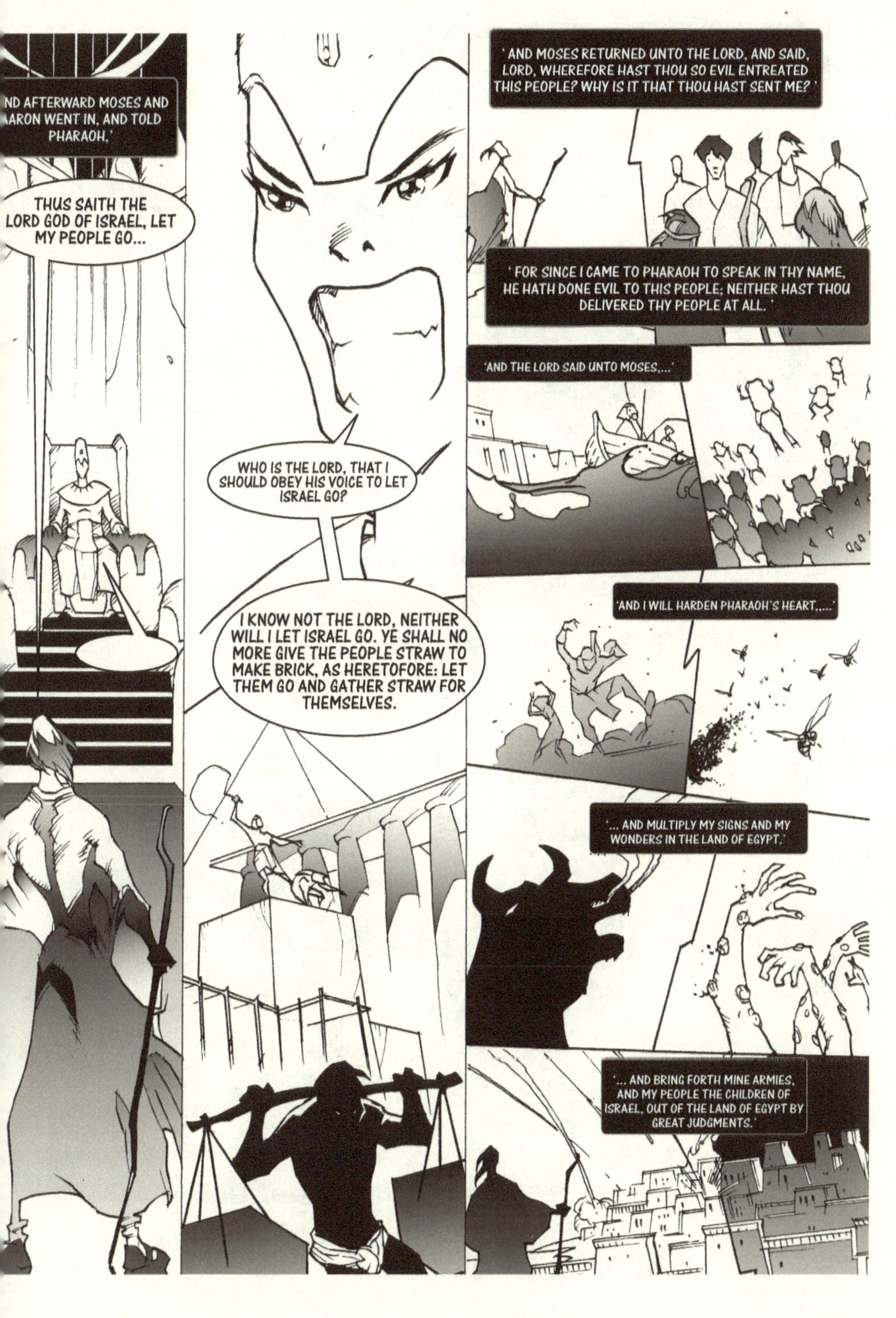
ND AFTERWARD MOSES AND
AARON WENT IN, AND TOLD
PHARAOH,'
THUS SAITH THE
LORD GOD OF ISRAEL, LET
MY PEOPLE GO...
WHO IS THE LORD, THAT I
SHOULD OBEY HIS VOICE TO LET
ISRAEL GO?
I KNOW NOT THE LORD, NEITHER
WILL I LET ISRAEL GO. YE SHALL NO
MORE GIVE THE PEOPLE STRAW TO
MAKE BRICK, AS HERETOFORE: LET
THEM GO AND GATHER STRAW FOR
THEMSELVES.
' AND MOSES RETURNED UNTO THE LORD, AND SAID,
LORD, WHEREFORE HAST THOU SO EVIL ENTREATED
THIS PEOPLE? WHY IS IT THAT THOU HAST SENT ME? '
' FOR SINCE I CAME TO PHARAOH TO SPEAK IN THY NAME,
HE HATH DONE EVIL TO THIS PEOPLE; NEITHER HAST THOU
DELIVERED THY PEOPLE AT ALL. '
'AND THE LORD SAID UNTO MOSES,...'
'AND I WILL HARDEN PHARAOH'S HEART,...'
'... AND MULTIPLY MY SIGNS AND MY
WONDERS IN THE LAND OF EGYPT.'
'... AND BRING FORTH MINE ARMIES,
AND MY PEOPLE THE CHILDREN OF
ISRAEL, OUT OF THE LAND OF EGYPT BY
GREAT JUDGMENTS.'

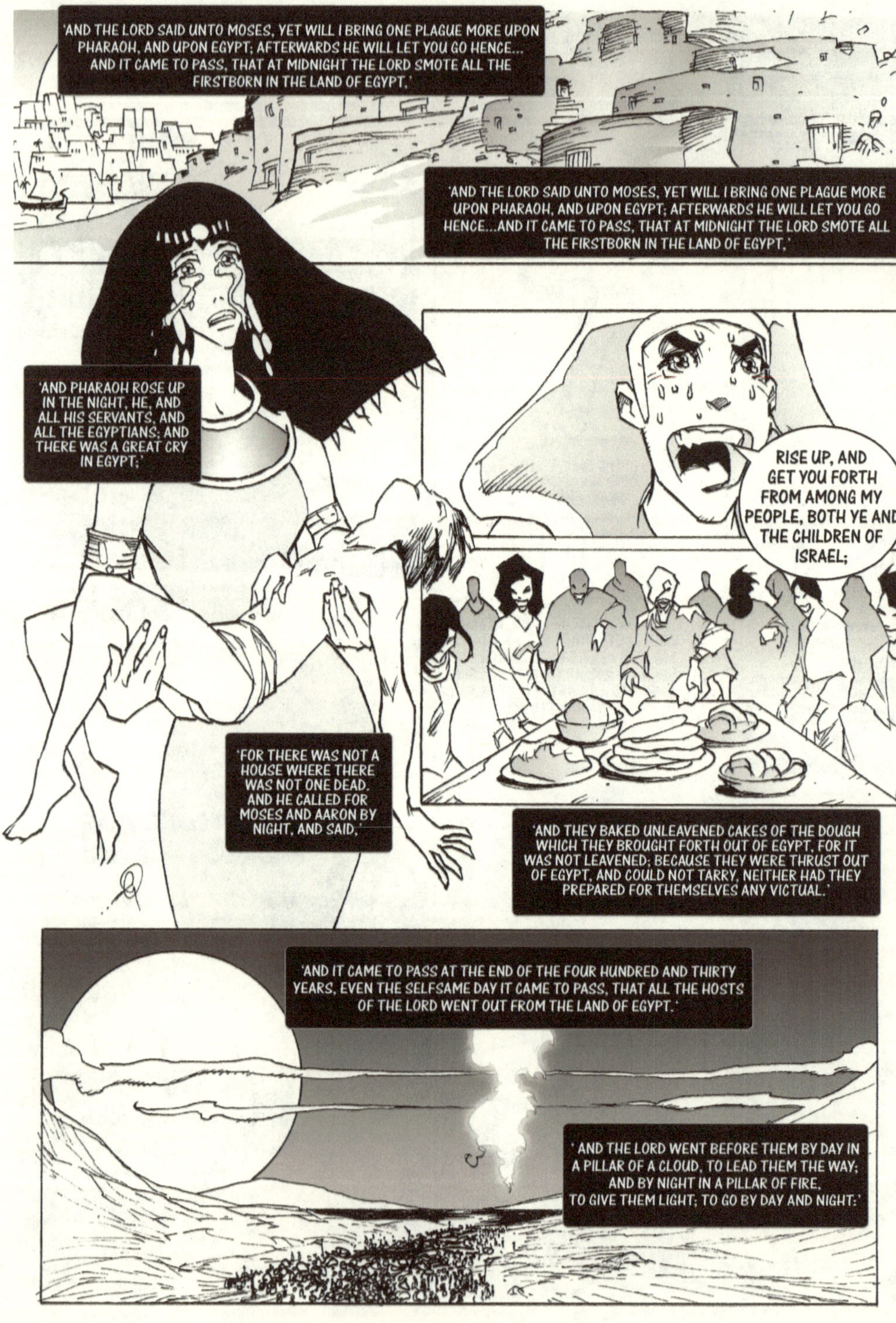
'AND THE LORD SAID UNTO MOSES, YET WILL I BRING ONE PLAGUE MORE UPON PHARAOH, AND UPON EGYPT; AFTERWARDS HE WILL LET YOU GO HENCE... AND IT CAME TO PASS, THAT AT MIDNIGHT THE LORD SMOTE ALL THE FIRSTBORN IN THE LAND OF EGYPT.'
'AND THE LORD SAID UNTO MOSES, YET WILL I BRING ONE PLAGUE MORE UPON PHARAOH, AND UPON EGYPT; AFTERWARDS HE WILL LET YOU GO HENCE...AND IT CAME TO PASS, THAT AT MIDNIGHT THE LORD SMOTE ALL THE FIRSTBORN IN THE LAND OF EGYPT.'
'AND PHARAOH ROSE UP IN THE NIGHT, HE, AND ALL HIS SERVANTS, AND ALL THE EGYPTIANS; AND THERE WAS A GREAT CRY IN EGYPT;'
'FOR THERE WAS NOT A HOUSE WHERE THERE WAS NOT ONE DEAD. AND HE CALLED FOR MOSES AND AARON BY NIGHT, AND SAID,'
RISE UP, AND GET YOU FORTH FROM AMONG MY PEOPLE, BOTH YE AND THE CHILDREN OF ISRAEL;
'AND THEY BAKED UNLEAVENED CAKES OF THE DOUGH WHICH THEY BROUGHT FORTH OUT OF EGYPT, FOR IT WAS NOT LEAVENED; BECAUSE THEY WERE THRUST OUT OF EGYPT, AND COULD NOT TARRY, NEITHER HAD THEY PREPARED FOR THEMSELVES ANY VICTUAL.'
'AND IT CAME TO PASS AT THE END OF THE FOUR HUNDRED AND THIRTY YEARS, EVEN THE SELFSAME DAY IT CAME TO PASS, THAT ALL THE HOSTS OF THE LORD WENT OUT FROM THE LAND OF EGYPT.'
'AND THE LORD WENT BEFORE THEM BY DAY IN A PILLAR OF A CLOUD, TO LEAD THEM THE WAY; AND BY NIGHT IN A PILLAR OF FIRE, TO GIVE THEM LIGHT; TO GO BY DAY AND NIGHT:'

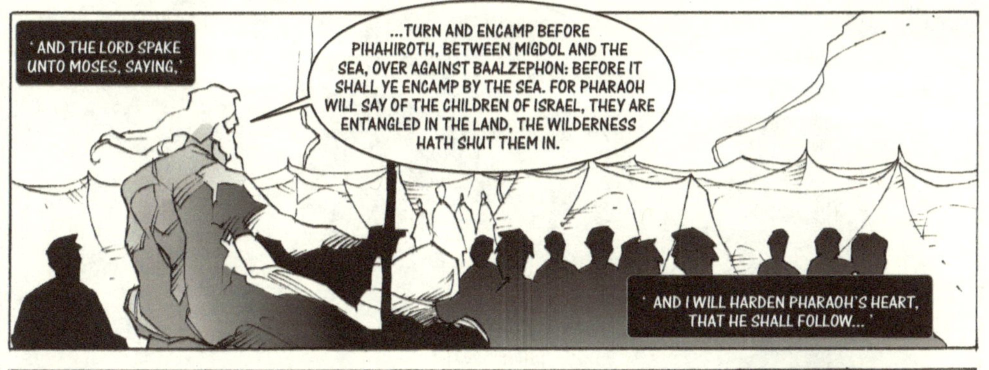

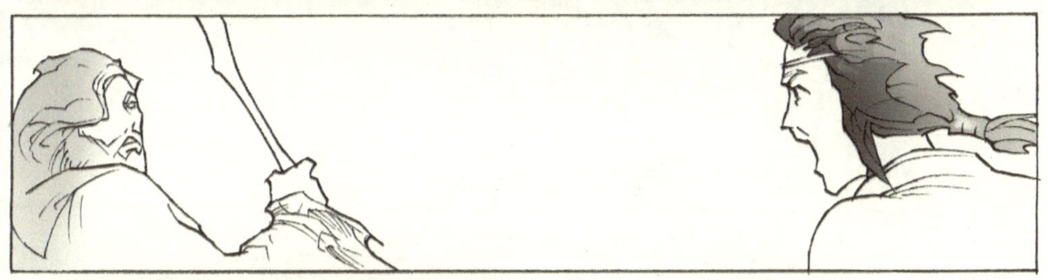

'AND IT WAS TOLD THE KING OF EGYPT THAT THE PEOPLE FLED: AND THE HEART OF PHARAOH AND OF HIS SERVANTS WAS TURNED AGAINST THE PEOPLE, AND THEY SAID, WHY HAVE WE DONE THIS, THAT WE HAVE LET ISRAEL GO FROM SERVING US? AND HE MADE READY HIS CHARIOT, AND TOOK HIS PEOPLE WITH HIM: AND HE TOOK SIX HUNDRED CHOSEN CHARIOTS, AND ALL THE CHARIOTS OF EGYPT, AND CAPTAINS OVER EVERY ONE OF THEM AND THE LORD HARDENED THE HEART OF PHARAOH KING OF EGYPT, AND HE PURSUED AFTER THE CHILDREN OF ISRAEL:'

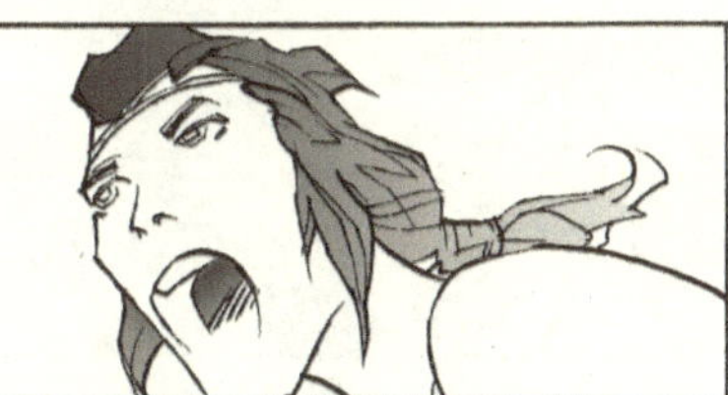

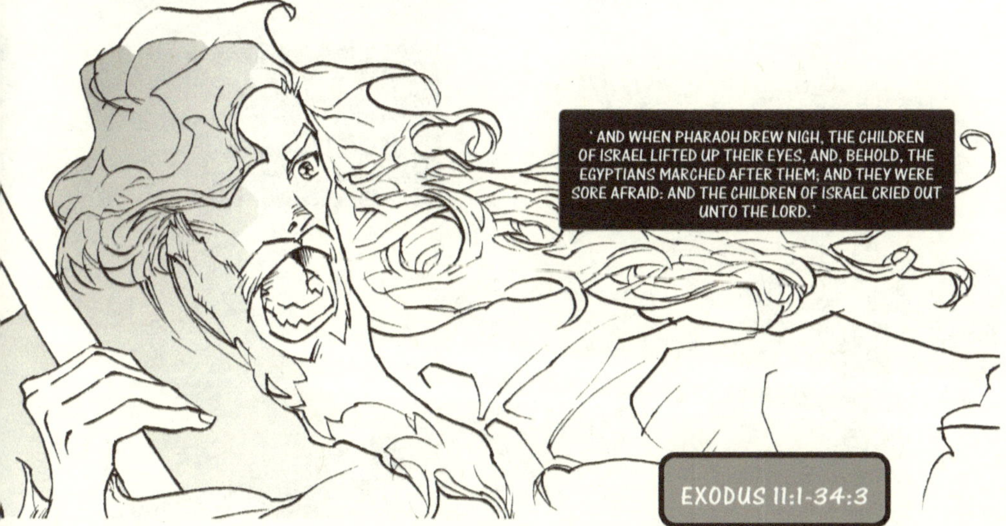

EXODUS 11:1-34:3

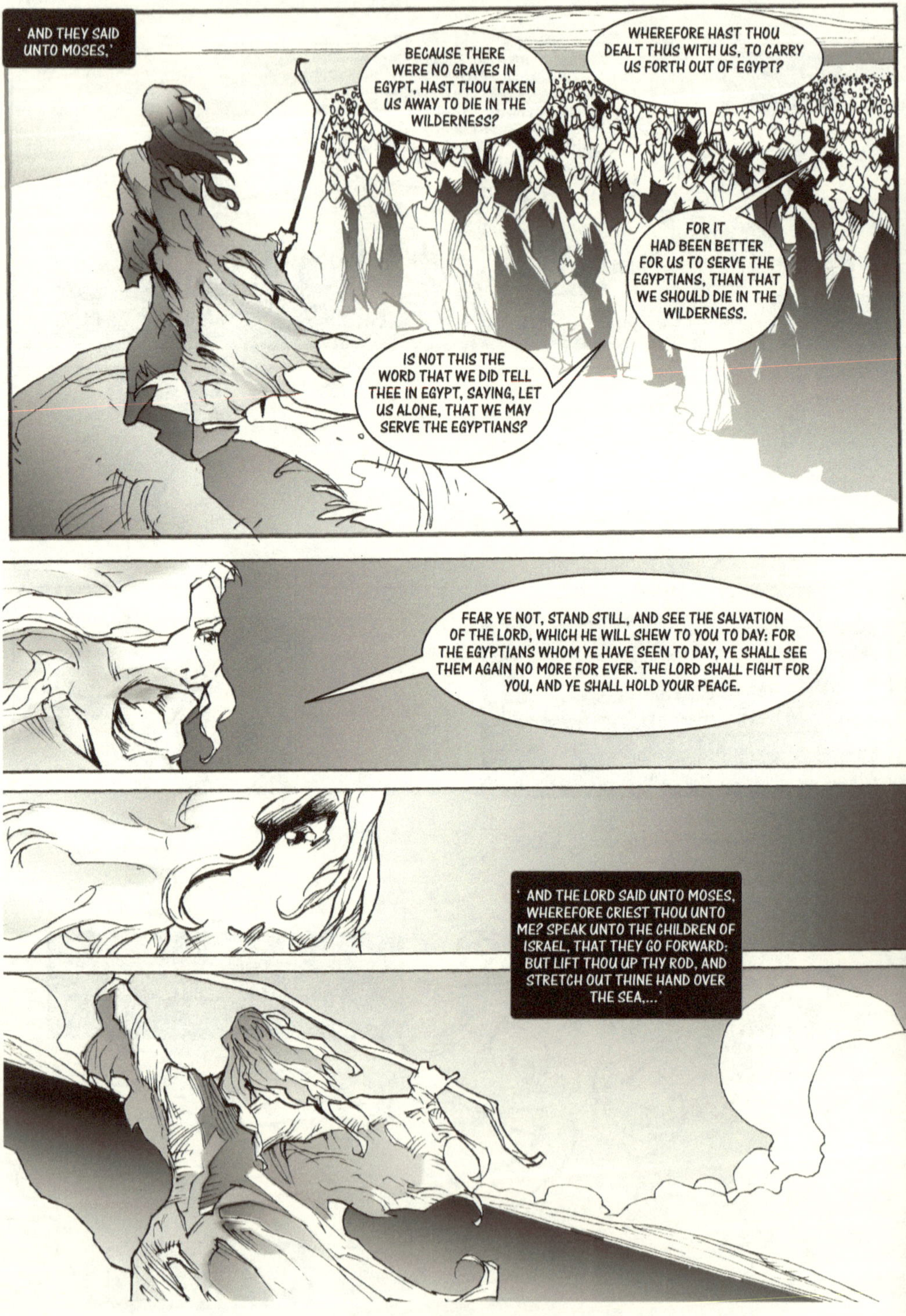

' AND THEY SAID UNTO MOSES,'

BECAUSE THERE WERE NO GRAVES IN EGYPT, HAST THOU TAKEN US AWAY TO DIE IN THE WILDERNESS?

WHEREFORE HAST THOU DEALT THUS WITH US, TO CARRY US FORTH OUT OF EGYPT?

IS NOT THIS THE WORD THAT WE DID TELL THEE IN EGYPT, SAYING, LET US ALONE, THAT WE MAY SERVE THE EGYPTIANS?

FOR IT HAD BEEN BETTER FOR US TO SERVE THE EGYPTIANS, THAN THAT WE SHOULD DIE IN THE WILDERNESS.

FEAR YE NOT, STAND STILL, AND SEE THE SALVATION OF THE LORD, WHICH HE WILL SHEW TO YOU TO DAY: FOR THE EGYPTIANS WHOM YE HAVE SEEN TO DAY, YE SHALL SEE THEM AGAIN NO MORE FOR EVER. THE LORD SHALL FIGHT FOR YOU, AND YE SHALL HOLD YOUR PEACE.

' AND THE LORD SAID UNTO MOSES, WHEREFORE CRIEST THOU UNTO ME? SPEAK UNTO THE CHILDREN OF ISRAEL, THAT THEY GO FORWARD: BUT LIFT THOU UP THY ROD, AND STRETCH OUT THINE HAND OVER THE SEA,...'

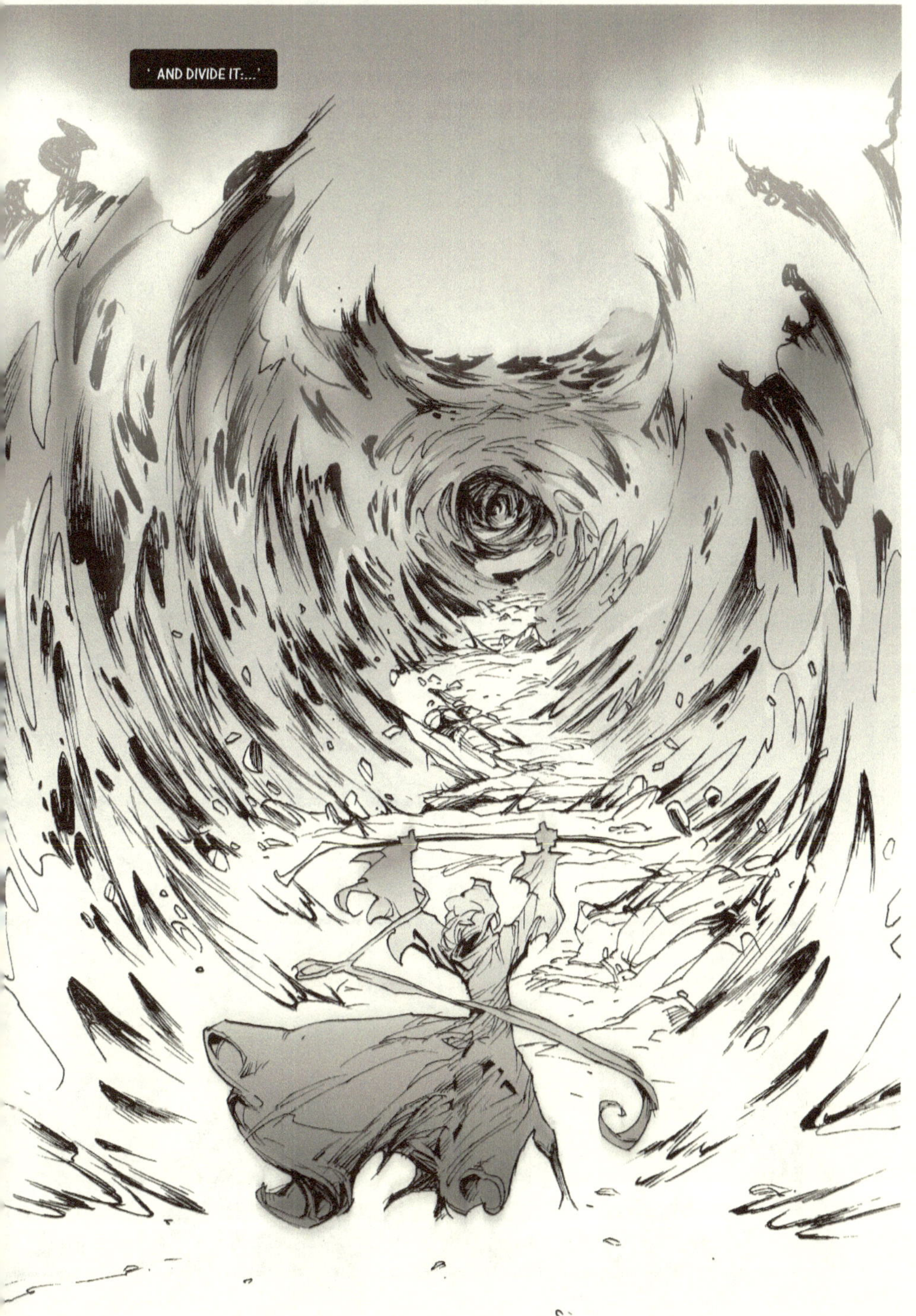
' AND DIVIDE IT:...'

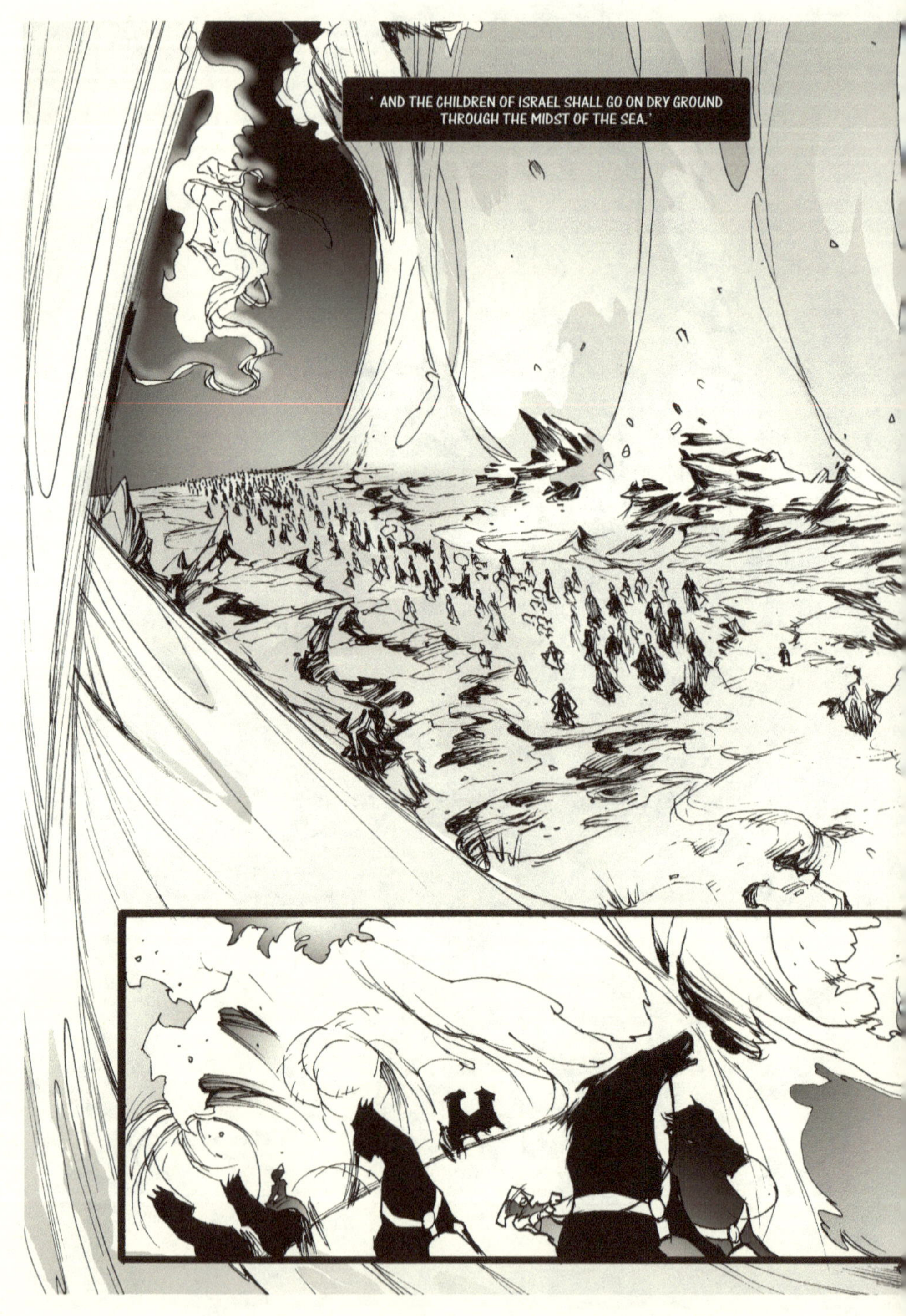
' AND THE CHILDREN OF ISRAEL SHALL GO ON DRY GROUND THROUGH THE MIDST OF THE SEA.'

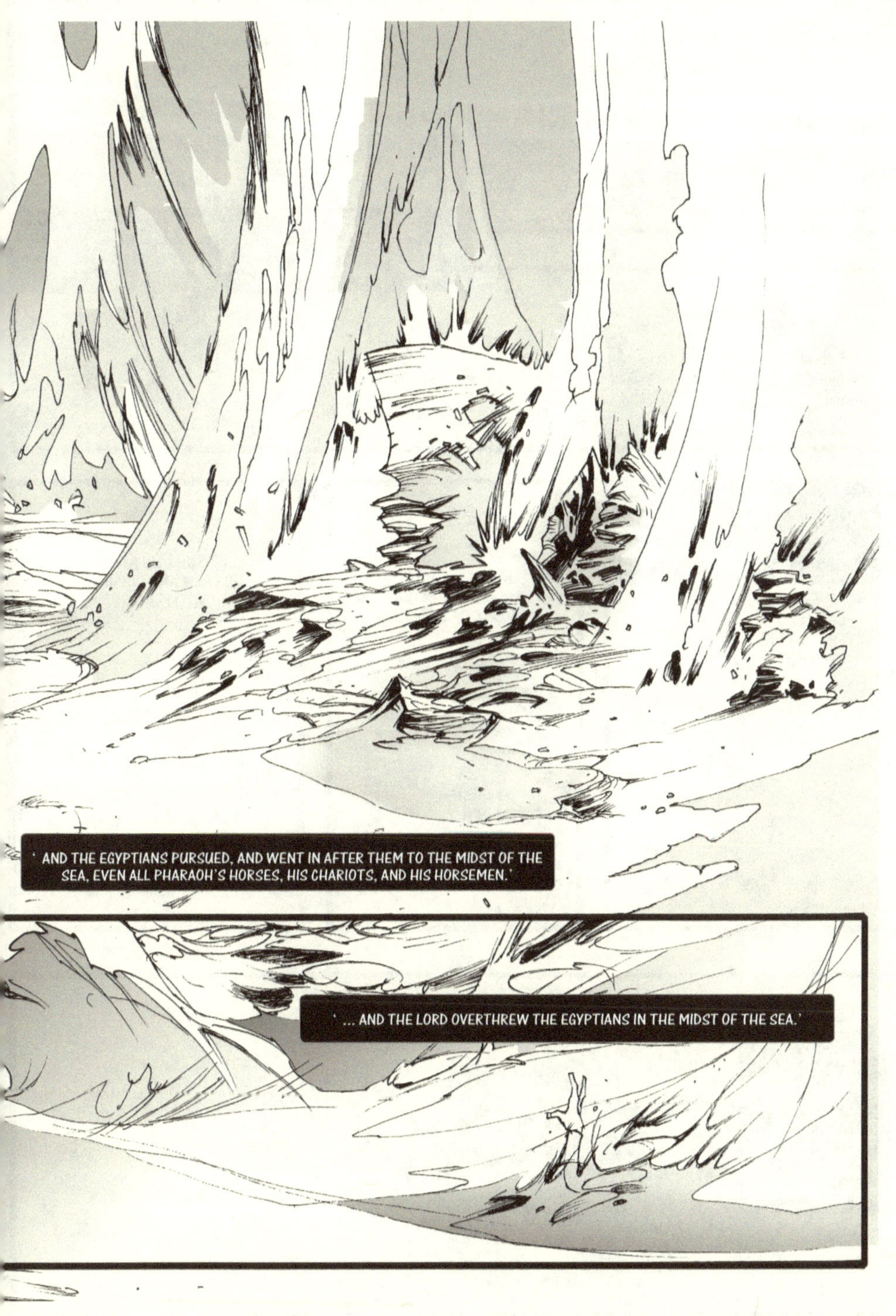
' AND THE EGYPTIANS PURSUED, AND WENT IN AFTER THEM TO THE MIDST OF THE SEA, EVEN ALL PHARAOH'S HORSES, HIS CHARIOTS, AND HIS HORSEMEN.'
' ... AND THE LORD OVERTHREW THE EGYPTIANS IN THE MIDST OF THE SEA.'

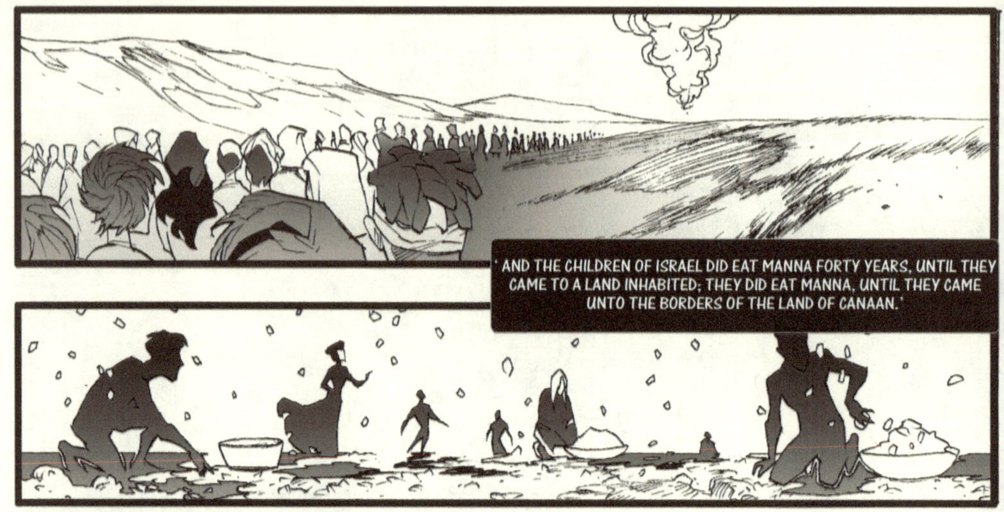
' AND THE CHILDREN OF ISRAEL DID EAT MANNA FORTY YEARS, UNTIL THEY CAME TO A LAND INHABITED; THEY DID EAT MANNA, UNTIL THEY CAME UNTO THE BORDERS OF THE LAND OF CANAAN.'

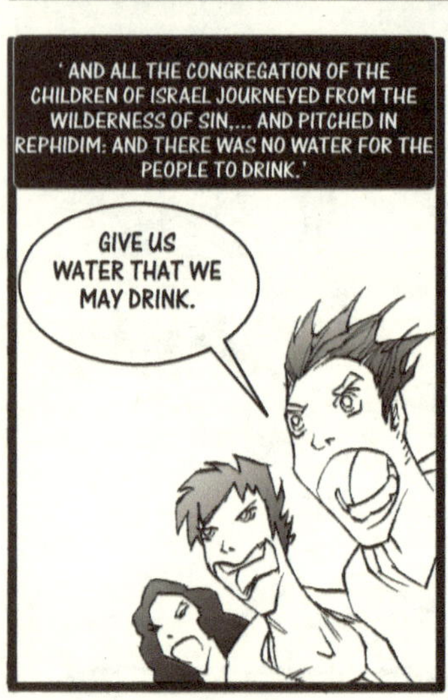
' AND ALL THE CONGREGATION OF THE CHILDREN OF ISRAEL JOURNEYED FROM THE WILDERNESS OF SIN,... AND PITCHED IN REPHIDIM: AND THERE WAS NO WATER FOR THE PEOPLE TO DRINK.'
GIVE US WATER THAT WE MAY DRINK.

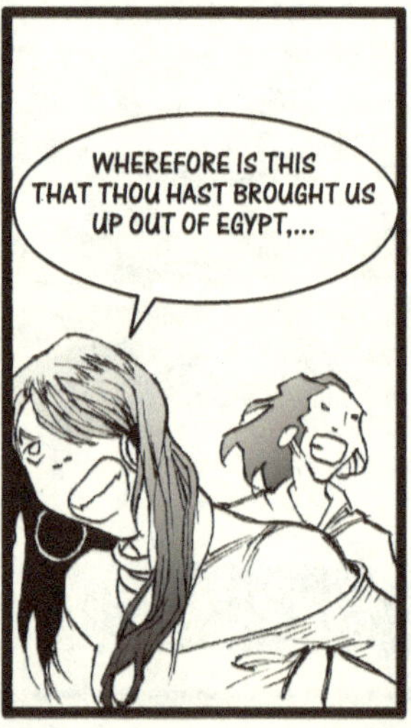
WHEREFORE IS THIS THAT THOU HAST BROUGHT US UP OUT OF EGYPT,...

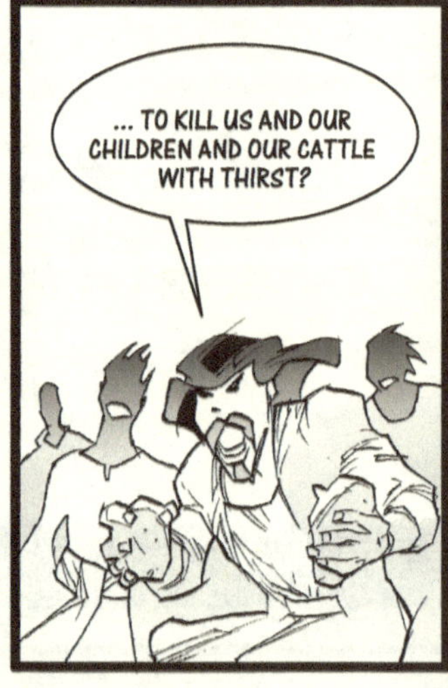
... TO KILL US AND OUR CHILDREN AND OUR CATTLE WITH THIRST?

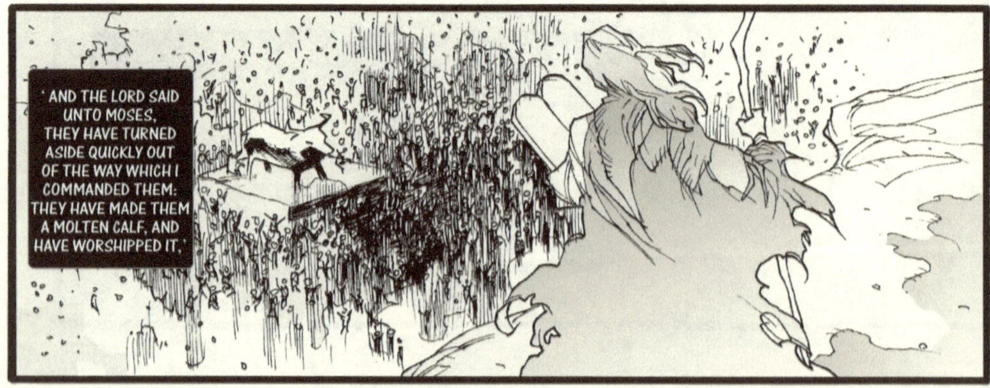
' AND THE LORD SAID UNTO MOSES, THEY HAVE TURNED ASIDE QUICKLY OUT OF THE WAY WHICH I COMMANDED THEM: THEY HAVE MADE THEM A MOLTEN CALF, AND HAVE WORSHIPPED IT.'

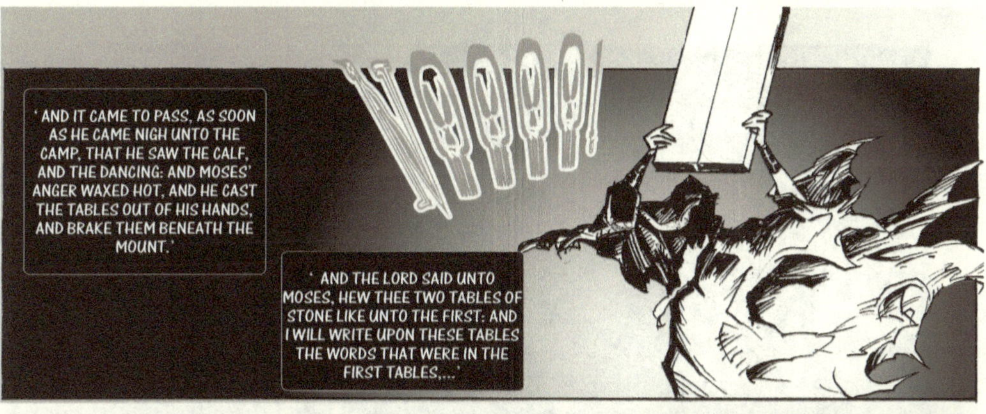

You shall have no other Gods but me | You shall worship no idols

You shall not misuse the Lord's name | You shall observe the Sabbath

You shall honour your father and mother | You shall not murder

You shall not commit adultery | You shall not steal

You shall not lie | You shall not covet your neighbours' property

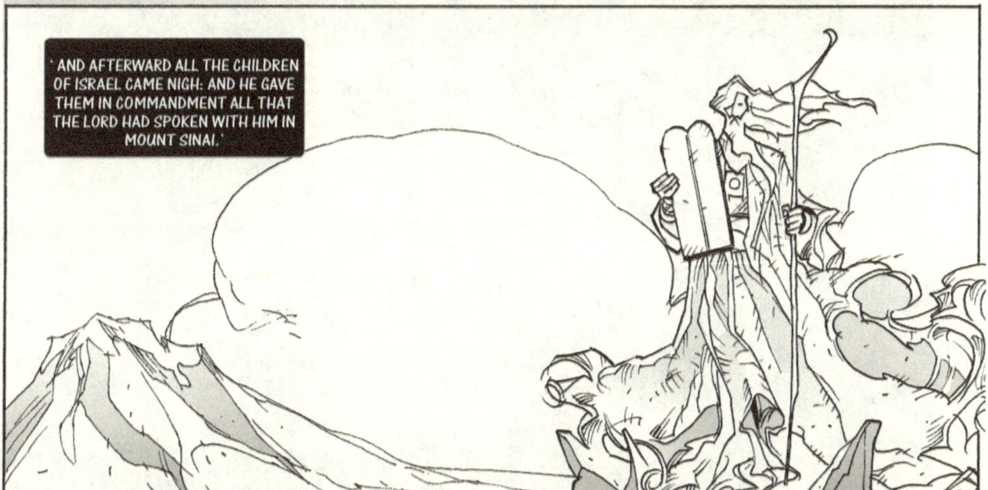

' AND AFTERWARD ALL THE CHILDREN OF ISRAEL CAME NIGH: AND HE GAVE THEM IN COMMANDMENT ALL THAT THE LORD HAD SPOKEN WITH HIM IN MOUNT SINAI.'

' AND I AM COME DOWN TO DELIVER THEM OUT OF THE HAND OF THE EGYPTIANS, AND TO BRING THEM UP OUT OF THAT LAND UNTO A GOOD LAND AND A LARGE, UNTO A LAND FLOWING WITH MILK AND HONEY...'

THE GOSPEL OF JESUS CHRIST

IN THE BEGINNING WAS THE WORD AND THE WORD WAS WITH GOD
AND THE WORD WAS GOD
THE SAME WAS IN THE BEGINNING WITH GOD
ALL THINGS WERE MADE BY HIM AND WITHOUT HIM WAS NOT ANY THING
MADE THAT WAS MADE
IN HIM WAS LIFE AND THE LIFE WAS THE LIGHT OF MEN
AND THE LIGHT SHINETH IN DARKNESS AND THE DARKNESS
COMPREHENDED IT NOT
THERE WAS A MAN SENT FROM GOD WHOSE NAME WAS JOHN
THE SAME CAME FOR A WITNESS TO BEAR WITNESS OF THE LIGHT THAT
ALL MEN THROUGH HIM MIGHT BELIEVE
HE WAS NOT THAT LIGHT BUT WAS SENT TO BEAR WITNESS
OF THAT LIGHT

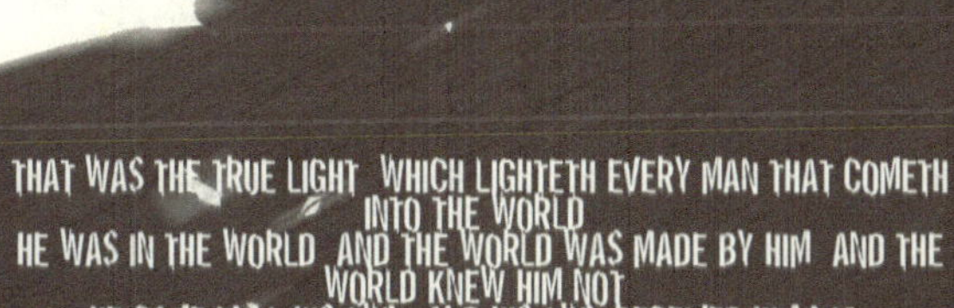

THAT WAS THE TRUE LIGHT WHICH LIGHTETH EVERY MAN THAT COMETH
INTO THE WORLD
HE WAS IN THE WORLD AND THE WORLD WAS MADE BY HIM AND THE
WORLD KNEW HIM NOT
HE CAME UNTO HIS OWN AND HIS OWN RECEIVED HIM NOT
BUT AS MANY AS RECEIVED HIM TO THEM GAVE HE POWER TO BECOME
THE SONS OF GOD EVEN TO THEM THAT BELIEVE ON HIS NAME
WHICH WERE BORN NOT OF BLOOD NOR OF THE WILL OF THE FLESH
NOR OF THE WILL OF MAN BUT OF GOD

AND THE WORD WAS MADE FLESH AND DWELT AMONG US AND WE
BEHELD HIS GLORY THE GLORY AS OF THE ONLY BEGOTTEN OF THE
FATHER FULL OF GRACE AND TRUTH
JOHN BARE WITNESS OF HIM AND CRIED SAYING THIS WAS HE OF WHOM
I SPAKE HE THAT COMETH AFTER ME IS PREFERRED BEFORE ME FOR HE
WAS BEFORE ME
AND OF HIS FULNESS HAVE ALL WE RECEIVED AND GRACE FOR GRACE
FOR THE LAW WAS GIVEN BY MOSES BUT GRACE AND TRUTH CAME BY
JESUS CHRIST

THE BAPTISM AND TEMPTATION OF JESUS

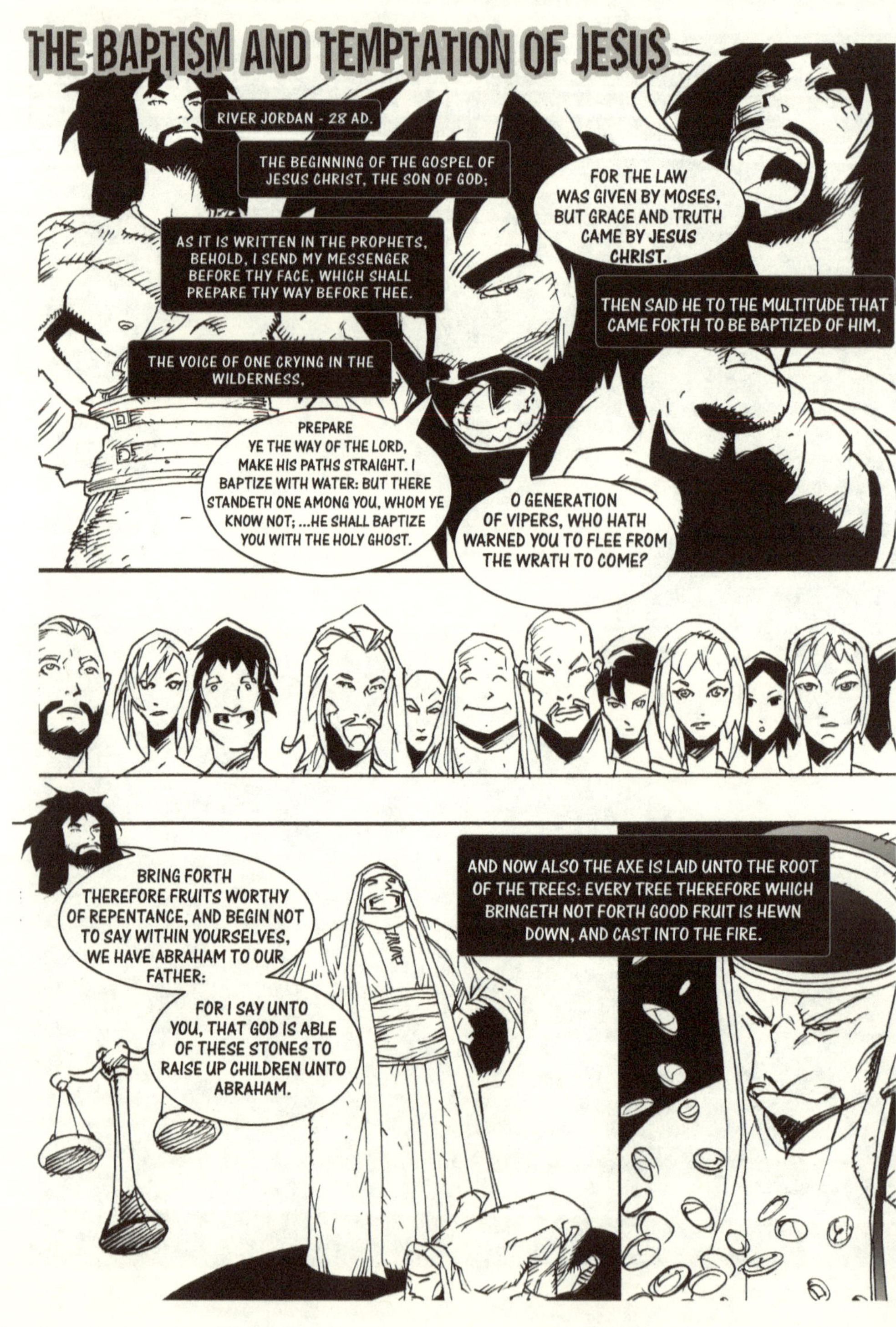

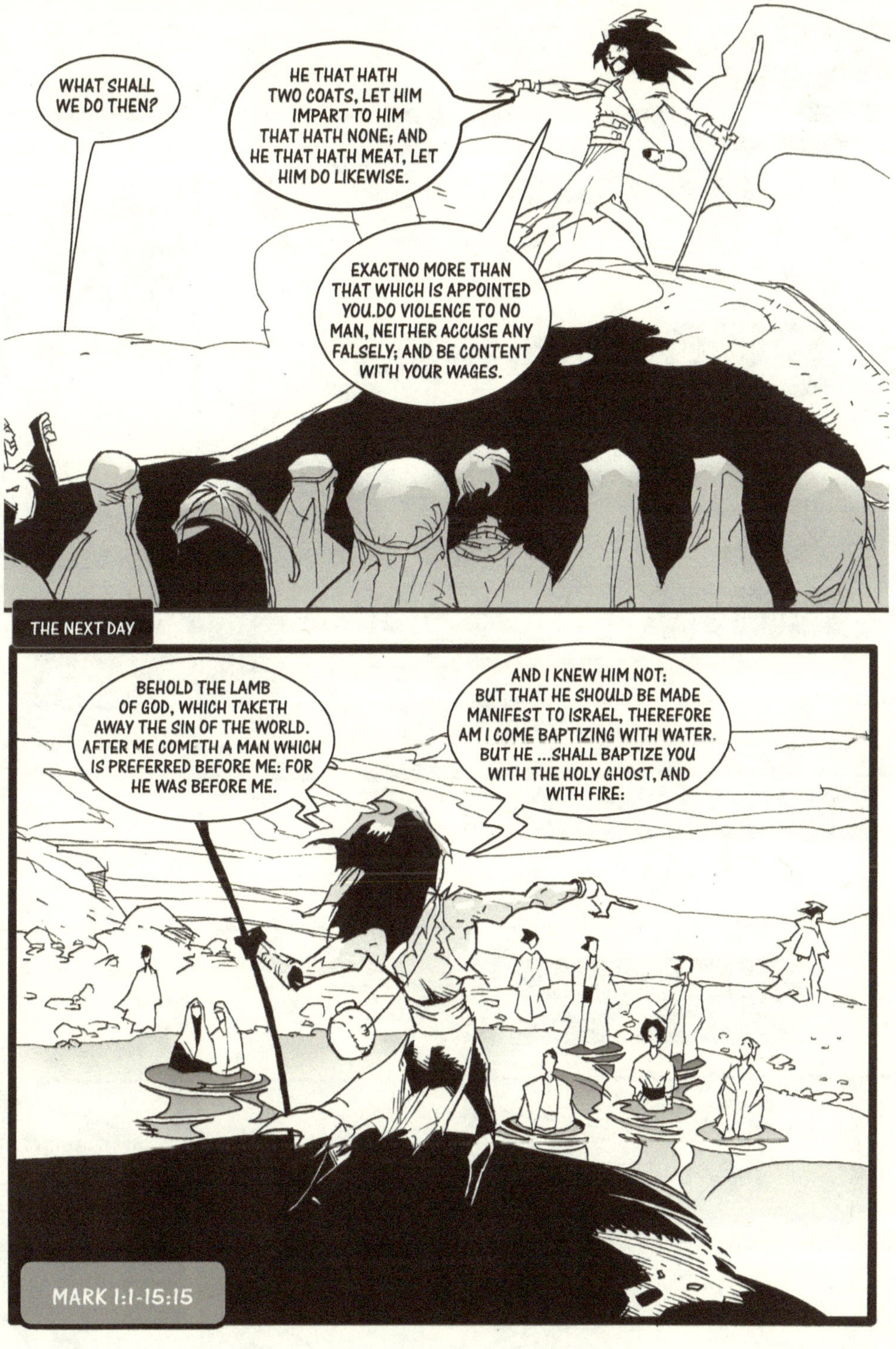
WHAT SHALL WE DO THEN?
HE THAT HATH TWO COATS, LET HIM IMPART TO HIM THAT HATH NONE; AND HE THAT HATH MEAT, LET HIM DO LIKEWISE.
EXACTNO MORE THAN THAT WHICH IS APPOINTED YOU.DO VIOLENCE TO NO MAN, NEITHER ACCUSE ANY FALSELY; AND BE CONTENT WITH YOUR WAGES.
THE NEXT DAY
BEHOLD THE LAMB OF GOD, WHICH TAKETH AWAY THE SIN OF THE WORLD. AFTER ME COMETH A MAN WHICH IS PREFERRED BEFORE ME: FOR HE WAS BEFORE ME.
AND I KNEW HIM NOT: BUT THAT HE SHOULD BE MADE MANIFEST TO ISRAEL, THEREFORE AM I COME BAPTIZING WITH WATER. BUT HE ...SHALL BAPTIZE YOU WITH THE HOLY GHOST, AND WITH FIRE:
MARK 1:1-15:15

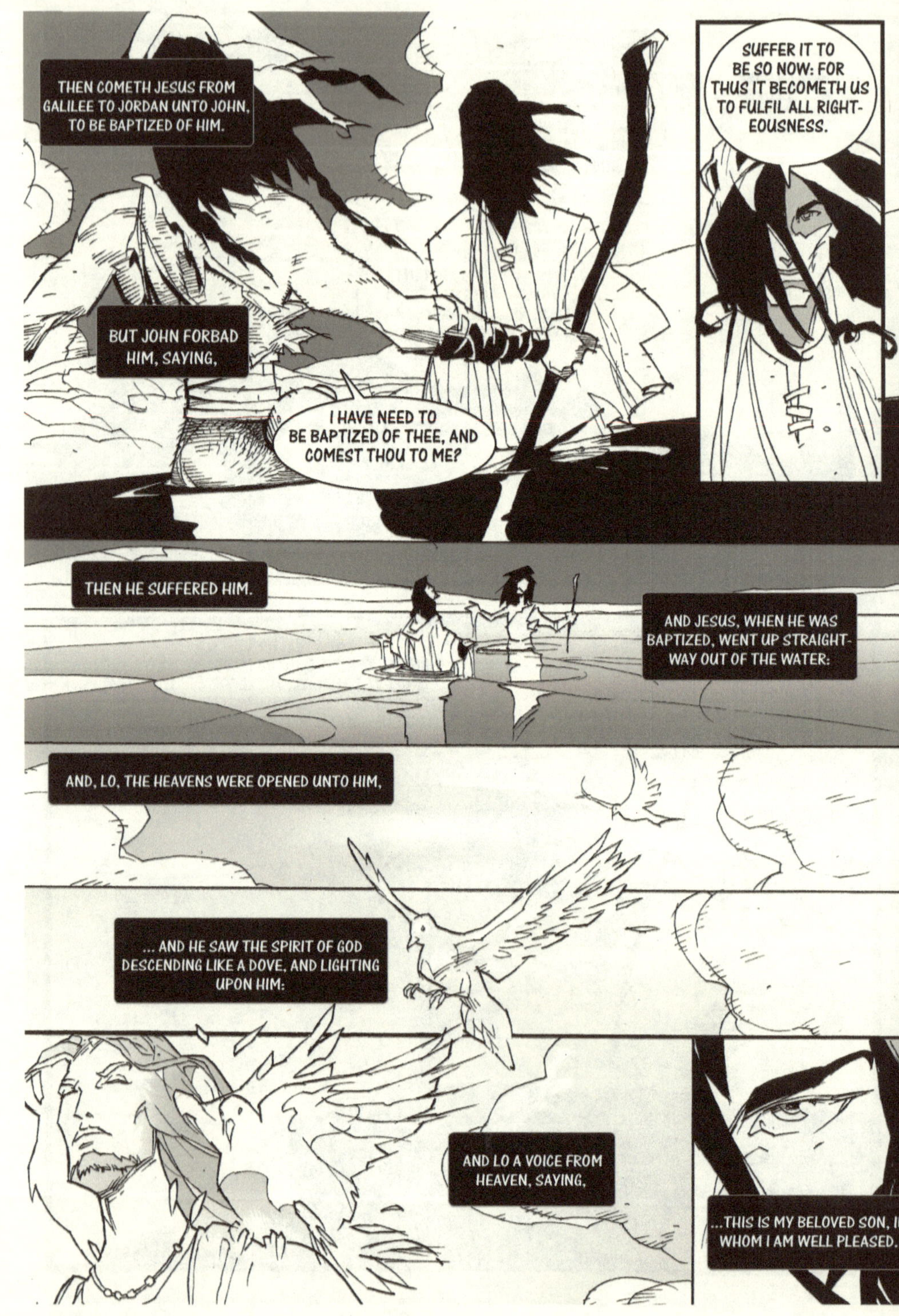
THEN COMETH JESUS FROM GALILEE TO JORDAN UNTO JOHN, TO BE BAPTIZED OF HIM.
BUT JOHN FORBAD HIM, SAYING,
I HAVE NEED TO BE BAPTIZED OF THEE, AND COMEST THOU TO ME?
SUFFER IT TO BE SO NOW: FOR THUS IT BECOMETH US TO FULFIL ALL RIGHT-EOUSNESS.
THEN HE SUFFERED HIM.
AND JESUS, WHEN HE WAS BAPTIZED, WENT UP STRAIGHT-WAY OUT OF THE WATER:
AND, LO, THE HEAVENS WERE OPENED UNTO HIM,
... AND HE SAW THE SPIRIT OF GOD DESCENDING LIKE A DOVE, AND LIGHTING UPON HIM:
AND LO A VOICE FROM HEAVEN, SAYING,
...THIS IS MY BELOVED SON, IN WHOM I AM WELL PLEASED.

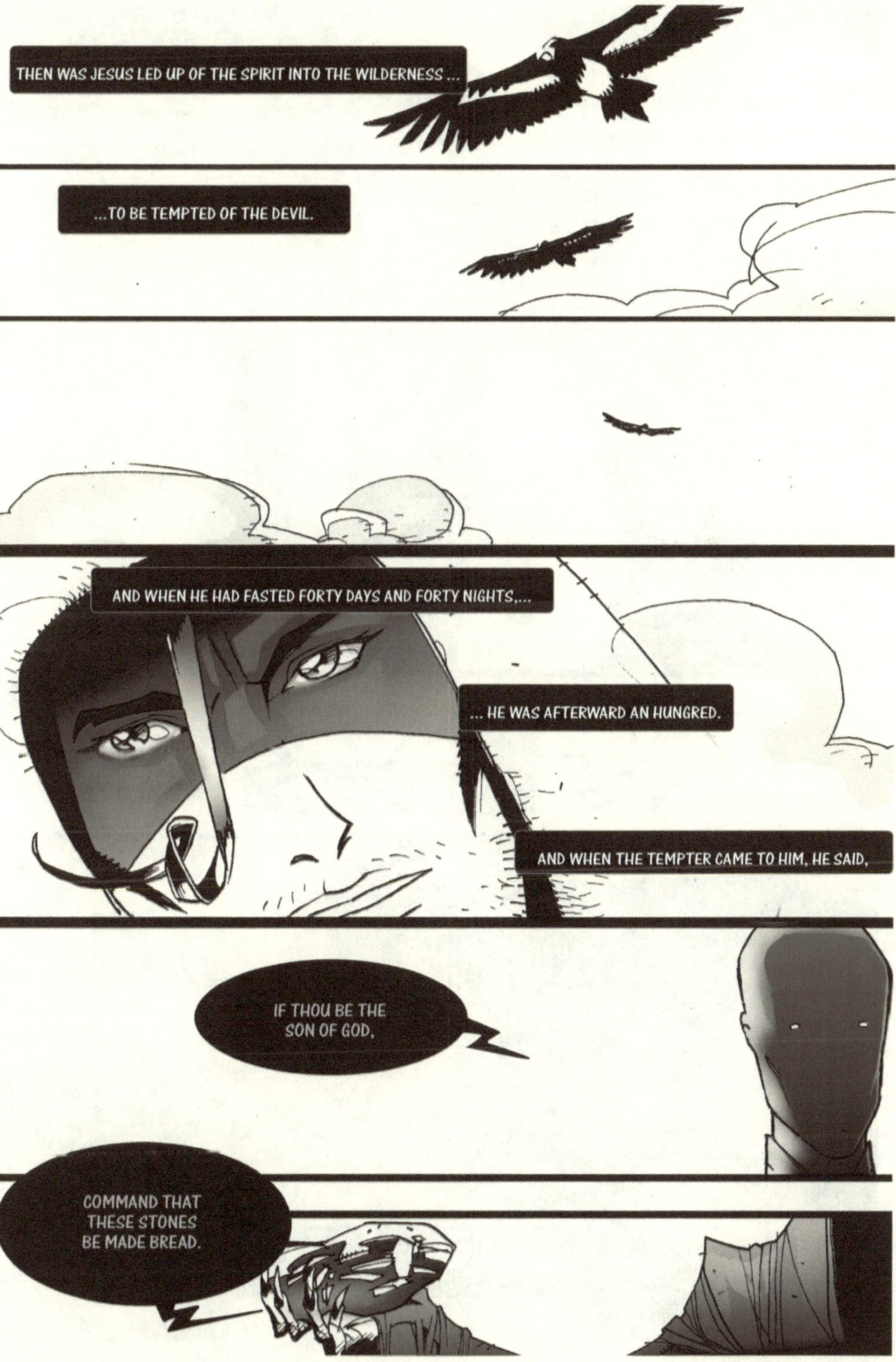
THEN WAS JESUS LED UP OF THE SPIRIT INTO THE WILDERNESS ...
...TO BE TEMPTED OF THE DEVIL.
AND WHEN HE HAD FASTED FORTY DAYS AND FORTY NIGHTS,...
... HE WAS AFTERWARD AN HUNGRED.
AND WHEN THE TEMPTER CAME TO HIM, HE SAID,
IF THOU BE THE SON OF GOD,
COMMAND THAT THESE STONES BE MADE BREAD.

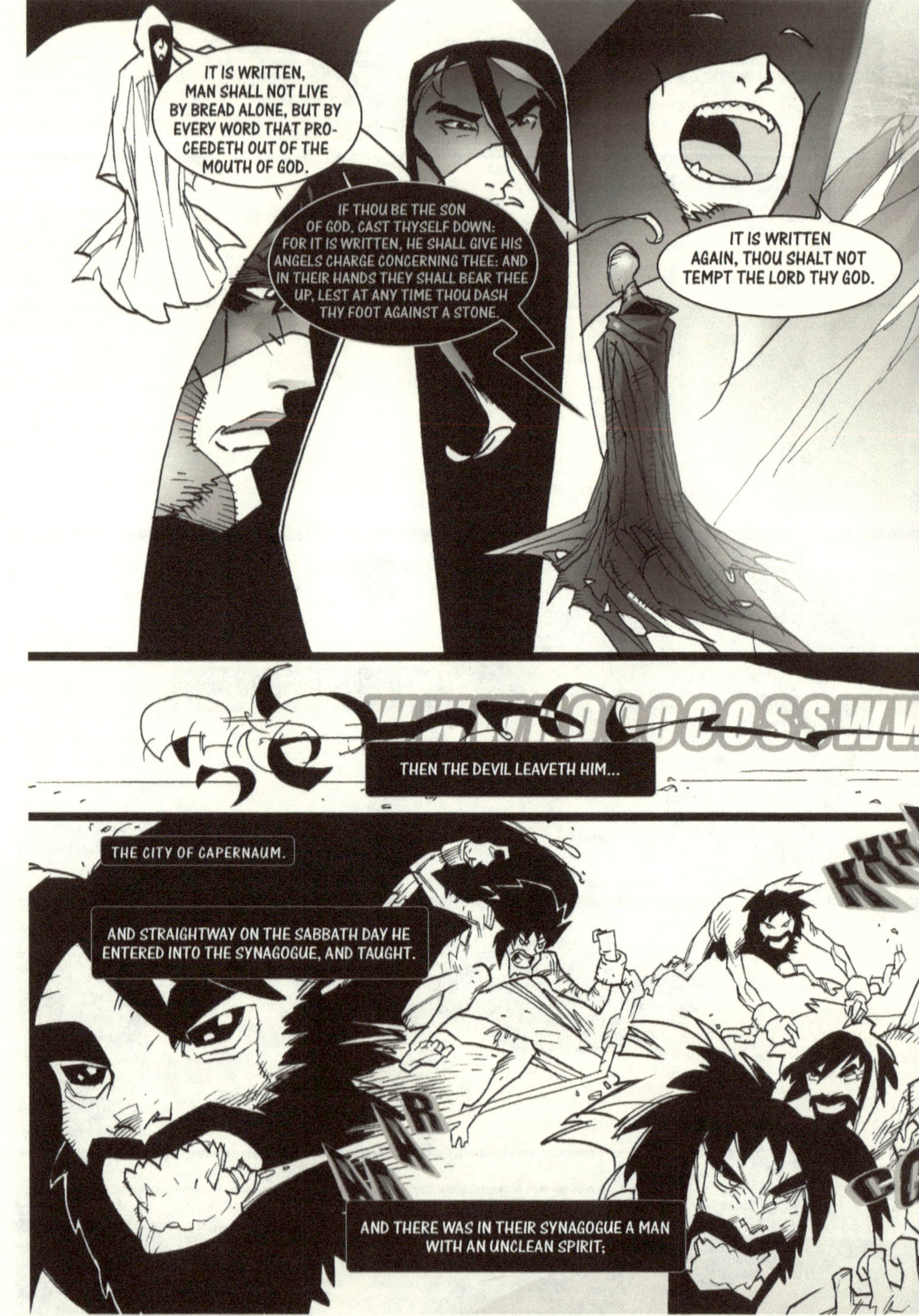

IT IS WRITTEN, MAN SHALL NOT LIVE BY BREAD ALONE, BUT BY EVERY WORD THAT PRO-CEEDETH OUT OF THE MOUTH OF GOD.
IF THOU BE THE SON OF GOD, CAST THYSELF DOWN: FOR IT IS WRITTEN, HE SHALL GIVE HIS ANGELS CHARGE CONCERNING THEE: AND IN THEIR HANDS THEY SHALL BEAR THEE UP, LEST AT ANY TIME THOU DASH THY FOOT AGAINST A STONE.
IT IS WRITTEN AGAIN, THOU SHALT NOT TEMPT THE LORD THY GOD.
THEN THE DEVIL LEAVETH HIM...
THE CITY OF CAPERNAUM.
AND STRAIGHTWAY ON THE SABBATH DAY HE ENTERED INTO THE SYNAGOGUE, AND TAUGHT.
AND THERE WAS IN THEIR SYNAGOGUE A MAN WITH AN UNCLEAN SPIRIT;

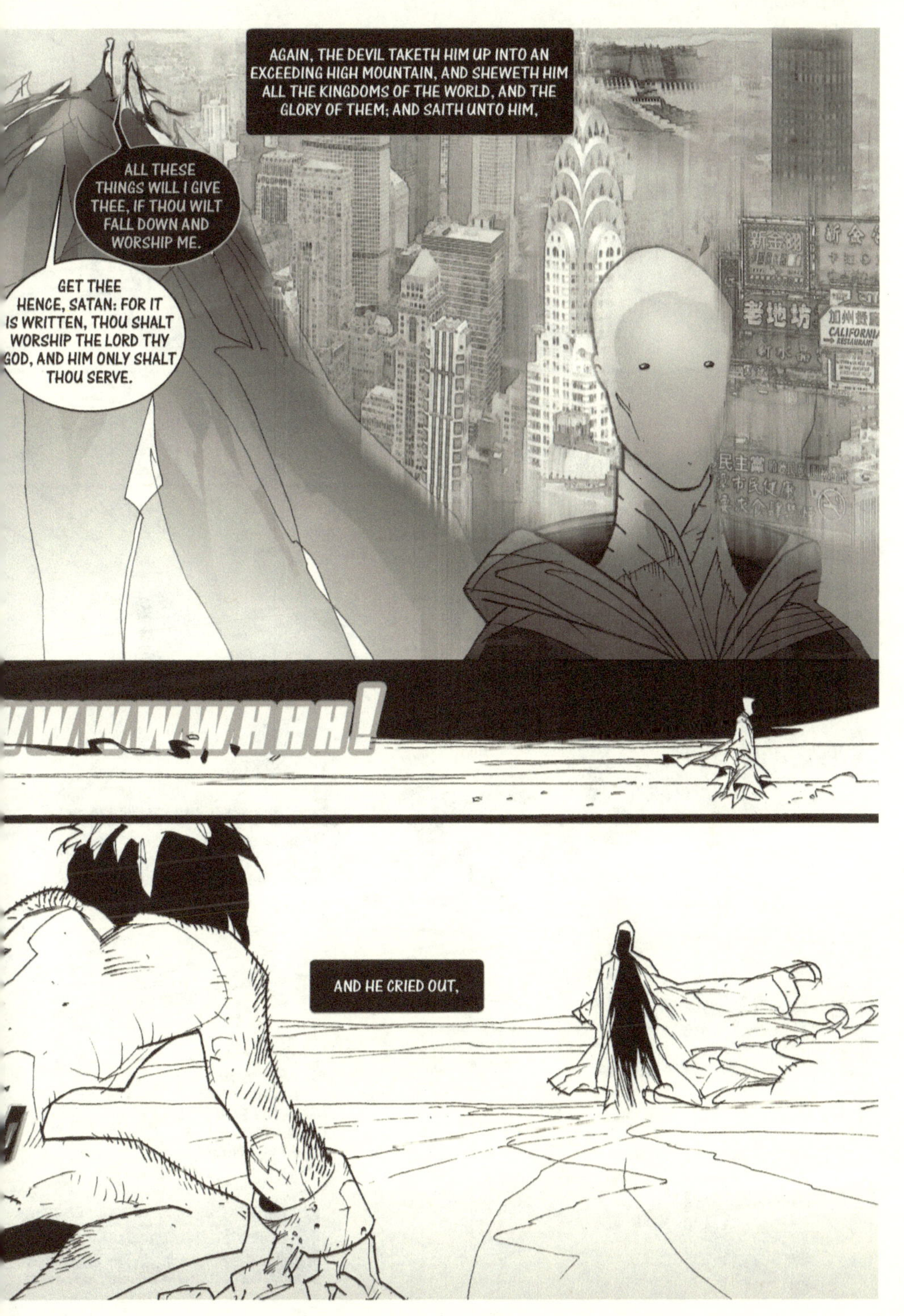
AGAIN, THE DEVIL TAKETH HIM UP INTO AN EXCEEDING HIGH MOUNTAIN, AND SHEWETH HIM ALL THE KINGDOMS OF THE WORLD, AND THE GLORY OF THEM; AND SAITH UNTO HIM,
ALL THESE THINGS WILL I GIVE THEE, IF THOU WILT FALL DOWN AND WORSHIP ME.
GET THEE HENCE, SATAN: FOR IT IS WRITTEN, THOU SHALT WORSHIP THE LORD THY GOD, AND HIM ONLY SHALT THOU SERVE.
老地坊
CALIFORNIA
WWWWHHH!
AND HE CRIED OUT,

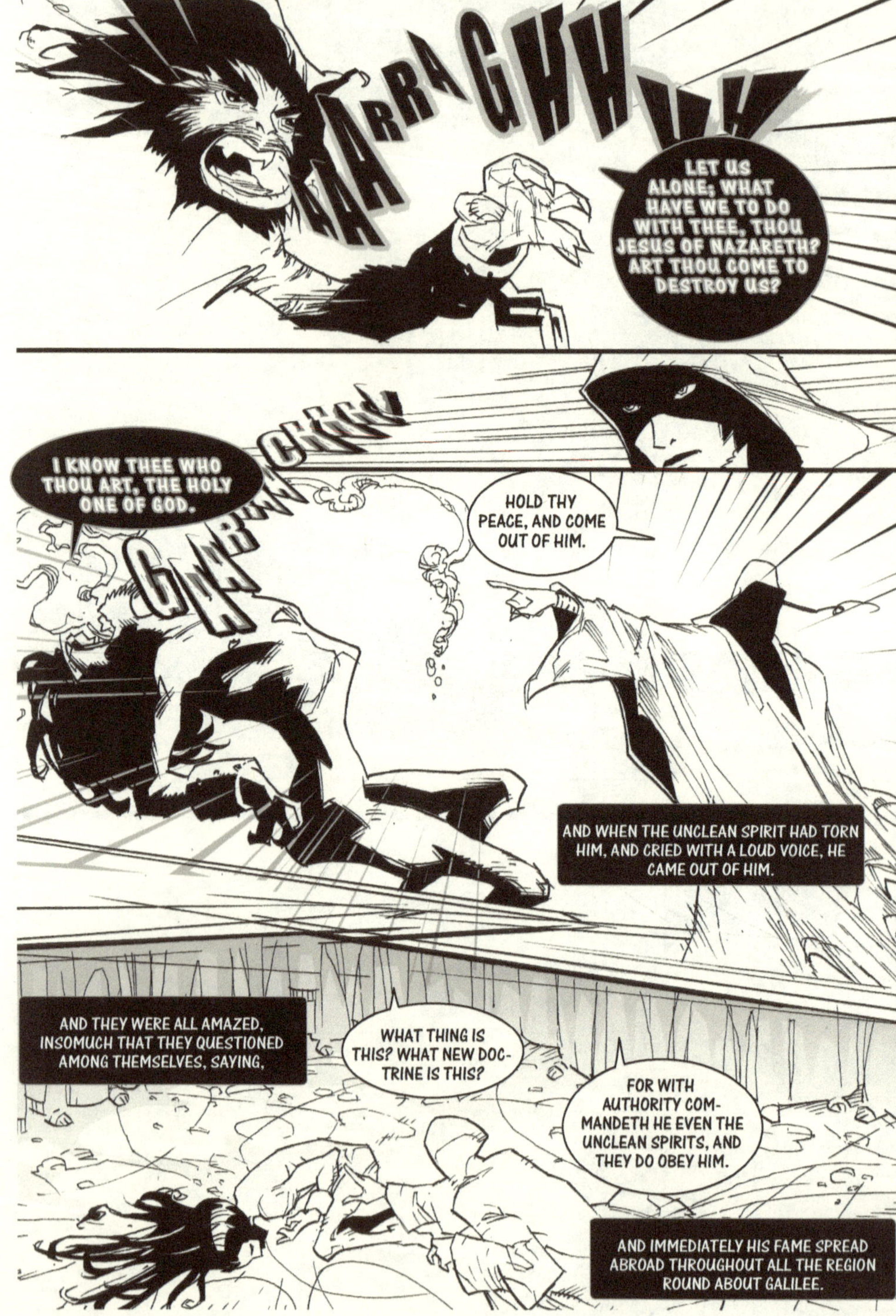

LET US ALONE; WHAT HAVE WE TO DO WITH THEE, THOU JESUS OF NAZARETH? ART THOU COME TO DESTROY US?
I KNOW THEE WHO THOU ART, THE HOLY ONE OF GOD.
HOLD THY PEACE, AND COME OUT OF HIM.
AND WHEN THE UNCLEAN SPIRIT HAD TORN HIM, AND CRIED WITH A LOUD VOICE, HE CAME OUT OF HIM.
AND THEY WERE ALL AMAZED, INSOMUCH THAT THEY QUESTIONED AMONG THEMSELVES, SAYING,
WHAT THING IS THIS? WHAT NEW DOC-TRINE IS THIS?
FOR WITH AUTHORITY COM-MANDETH HE EVEN THE UNCLEAN SPIRITS, AND THEY DO OBEY HIM.
AND IMMEDIATELY HIS FAME SPREAD ABROAD THROUGHOUT ALL THE REGION ROUND ABOUT GALILEE.

THE PARABLES OF JESUS

THE GOOD SAMARITAN

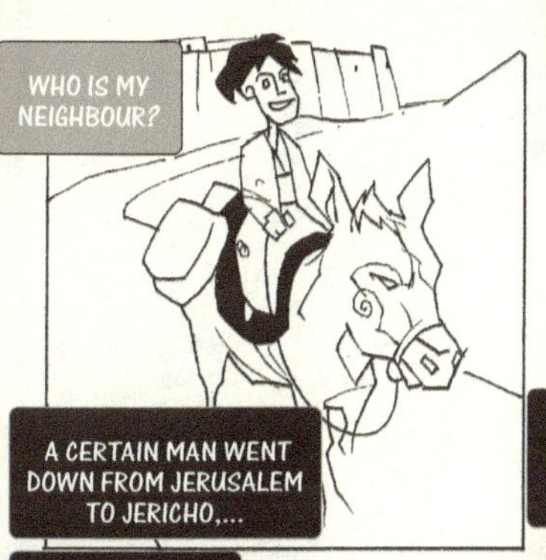

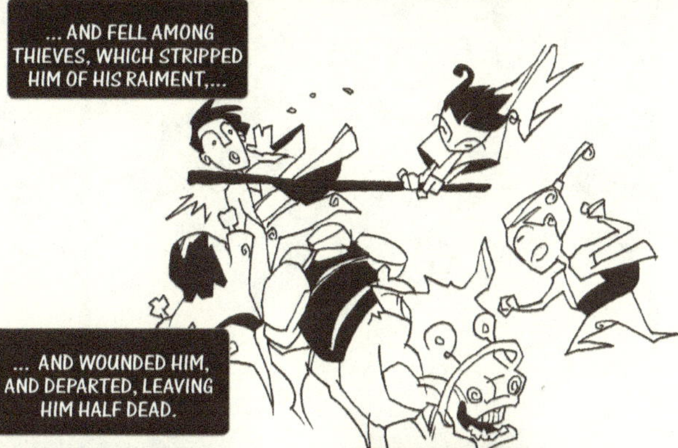

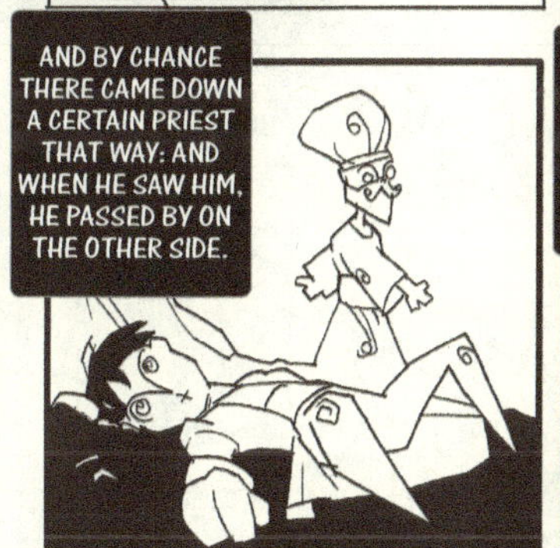

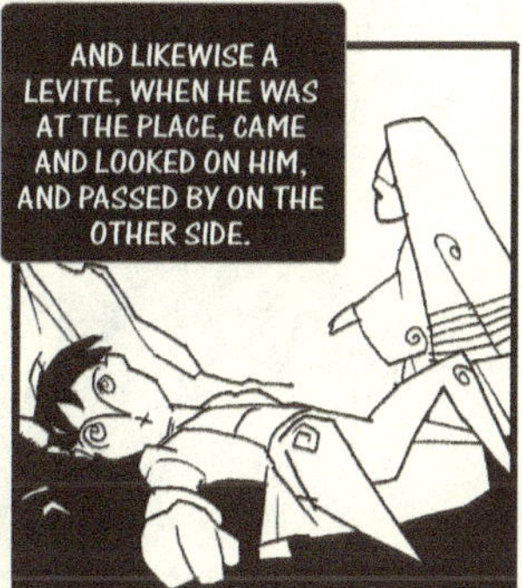

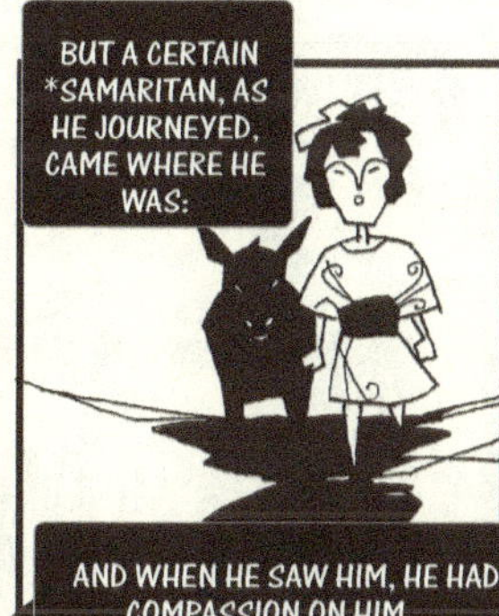

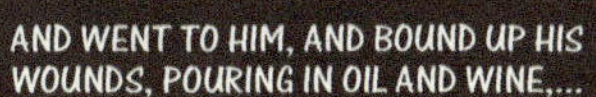

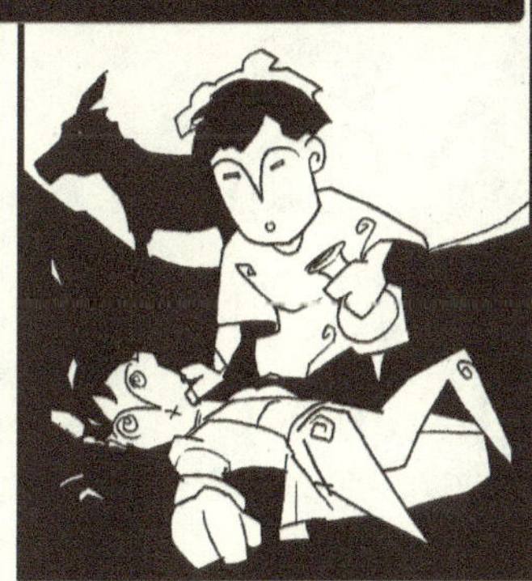

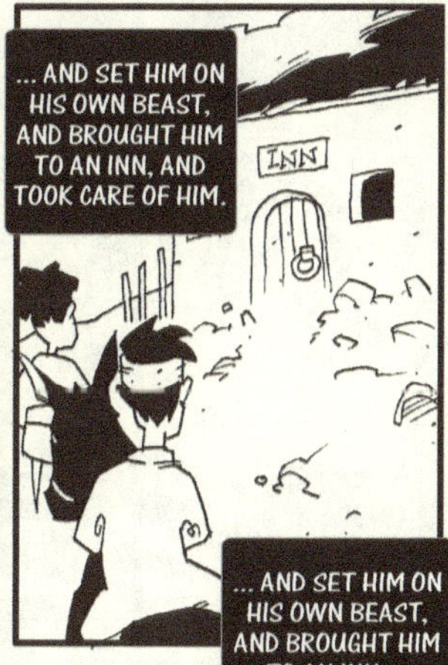

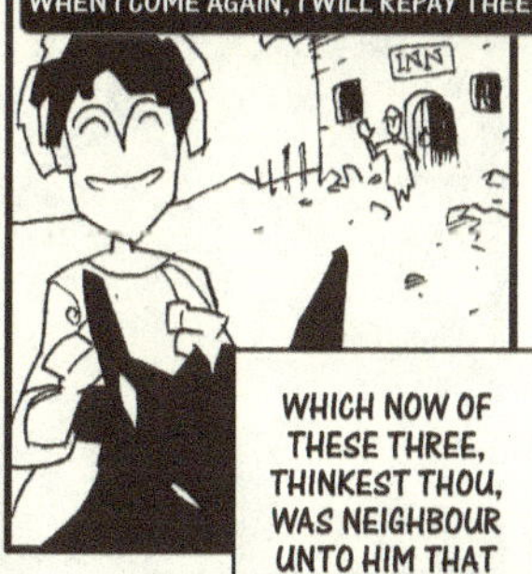

*AN UNTOUCHABLE.

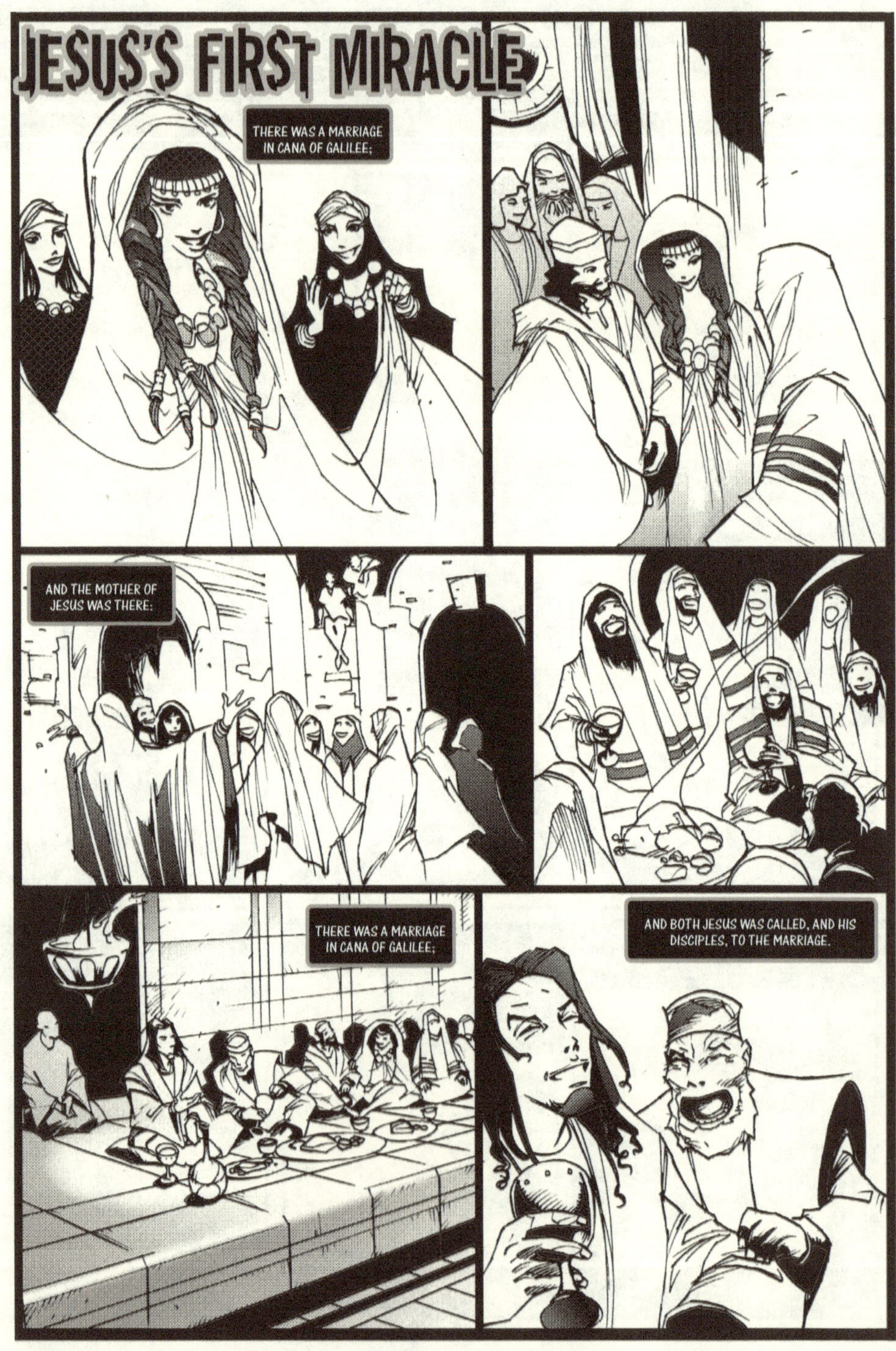
JESUS'S FIRST MIRACLE
THERE WAS A MARRIAGE IN CANA OF GALILEE;
AND THE MOTHER OF JESUS WAS THERE:
THERE WAS A MARRIAGE IN CANA OF GALILEE;
AND BOTH JESUS WAS CALLED, AND HIS DISCIPLES, TO THE MARRIAGE.

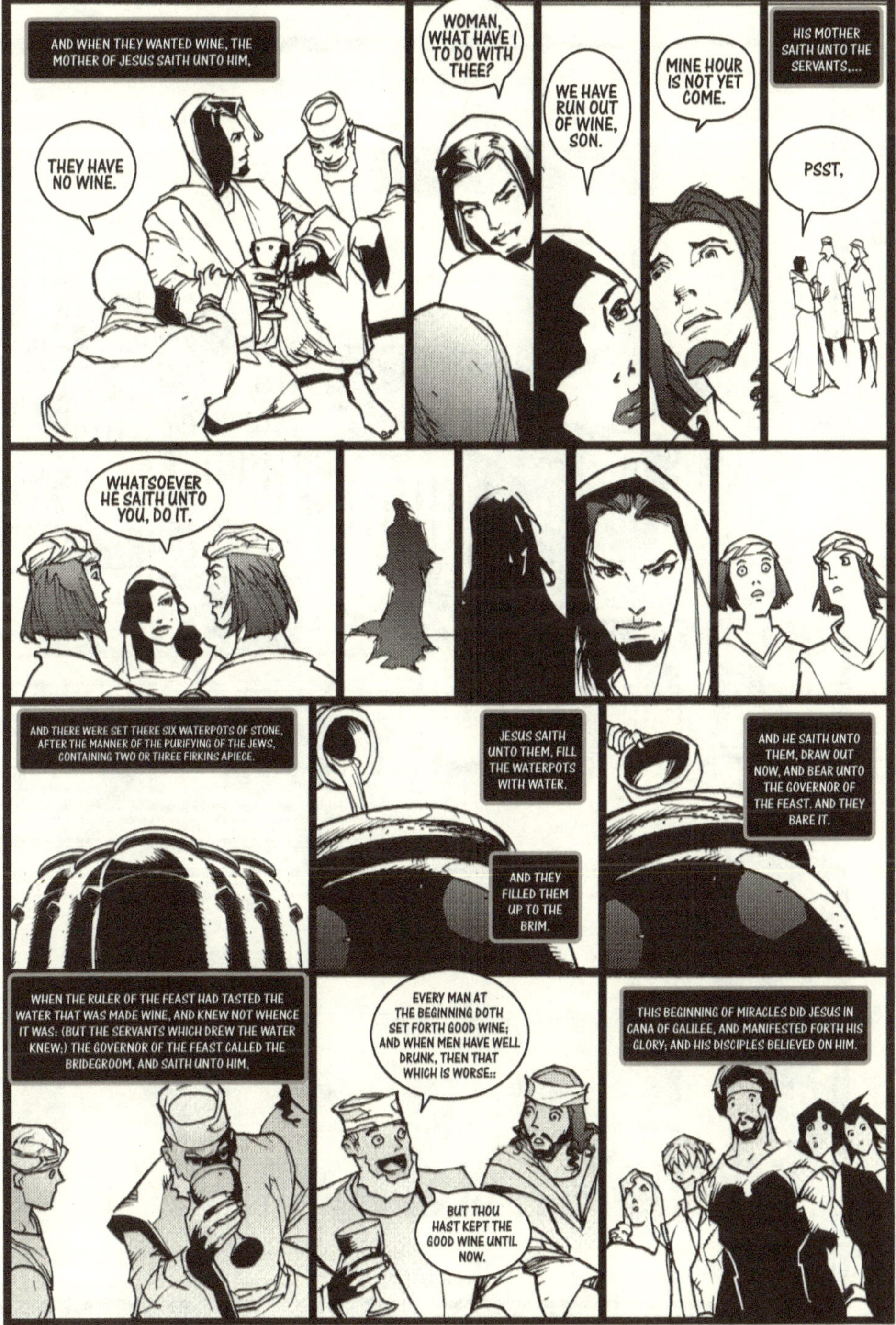
AND WHEN THEY WANTED WINE, THE MOTHER OF JESUS SAITH UNTO HIM,
THEY HAVE NO WINE.
WOMAN, WHAT HAVE I TO DO WITH THEE?
WE HAVE RUN OUT OF WINE, SON.
MINE HOUR IS NOT YET COME.
HIS MOTHER SAITH UNTO THE SERVANTS,...
PSST,
WHATSOEVER HE SAITH UNTO YOU, DO IT.
AND THERE WERE SET THERE SIX WATERPOTS OF STONE, AFTER THE MANNER OF THE PURIFYING OF THE JEWS, CONTAINING TWO OR THREE FIRKINS APIECE.
JESUS SAITH UNTO THEM, FILL THE WATERPOTS WITH WATER.
AND THEY FILLED THEM UP TO THE BRIM.
AND HE SAITH UNTO THEM, DRAW OUT NOW, AND BEAR UNTO THE GOVERNOR OF THE FEAST. AND THEY BARE IT.
WHEN THE RULER OF THE FEAST HAD TASTED THE WATER THAT WAS MADE WINE, AND KNEW NOT WHENCE IT WAS: (BUT THE SERVANTS WHICH DREW THE WATER KNEW;) THE GOVERNOR OF THE FEAST CALLED THE BRIDEGROOM, AND SAITH UNTO HIM,
EVERY MAN AT THE BEGINNING DOTH SET FORTH GOOD WINE; AND WHEN MEN HAVE WELL DRUNK, THEN THAT WHICH IS WORSE::
BUT THOU HAST KEPT THE GOOD WINE UNTIL NOW.
THIS BEGINNING OF MIRACLES DID JESUS IN CANA OF GALILEE, AND MANIFESTED FORTH HIS GLORY; AND HIS DISCIPLES BELIEVED ON HIM.

AND THE JEWS' PASSOVER WAS AT HAND, ...

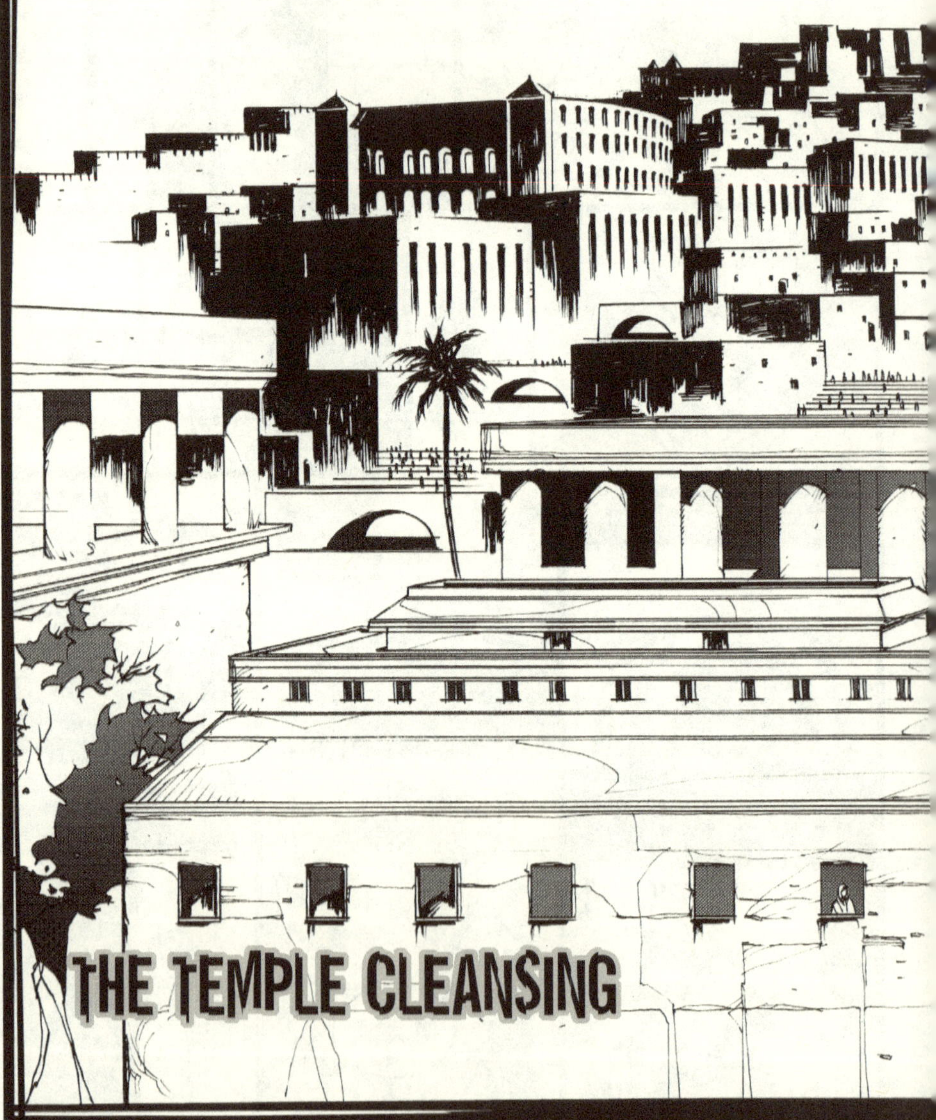

THE TEMPLE CLEANSING

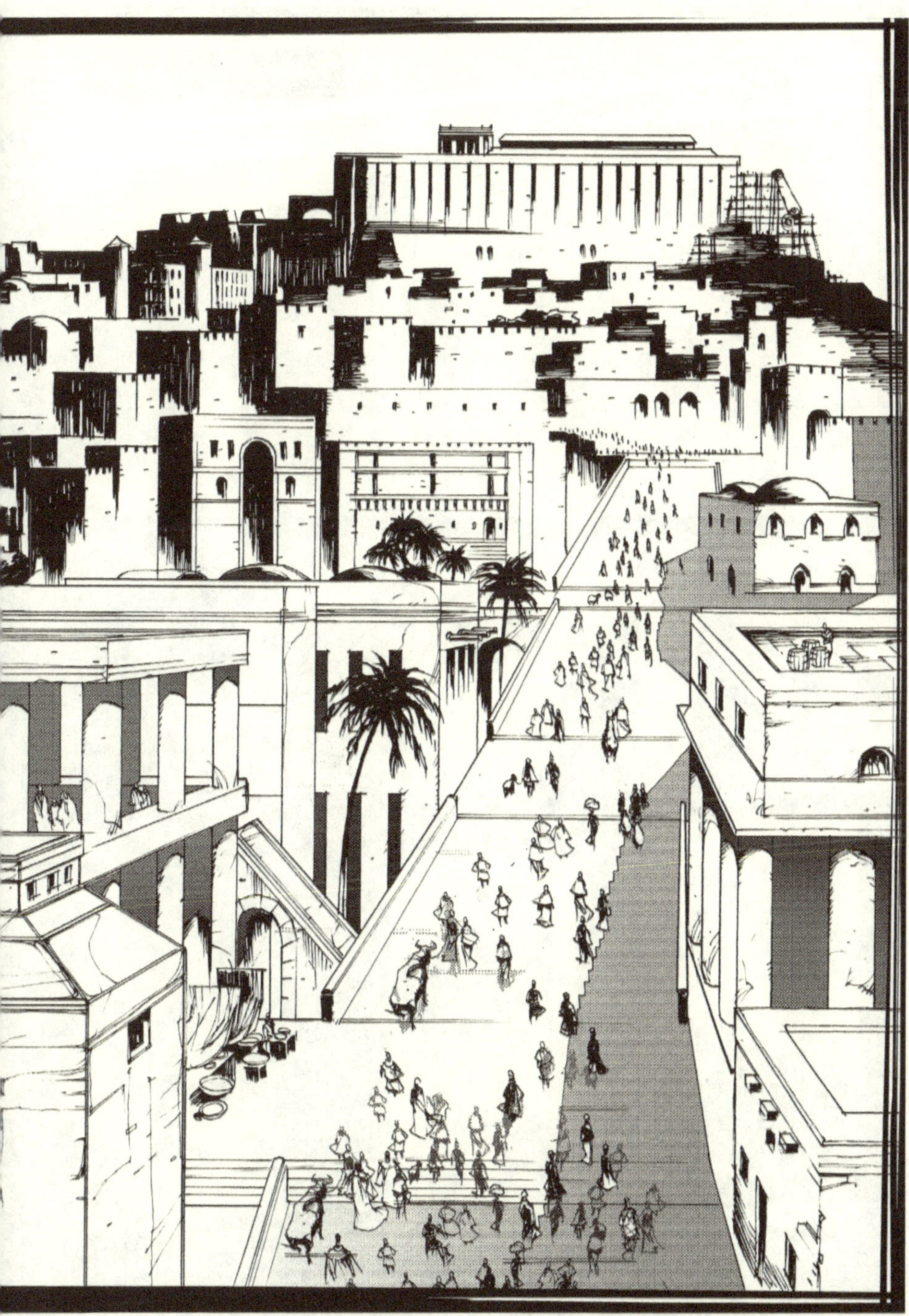

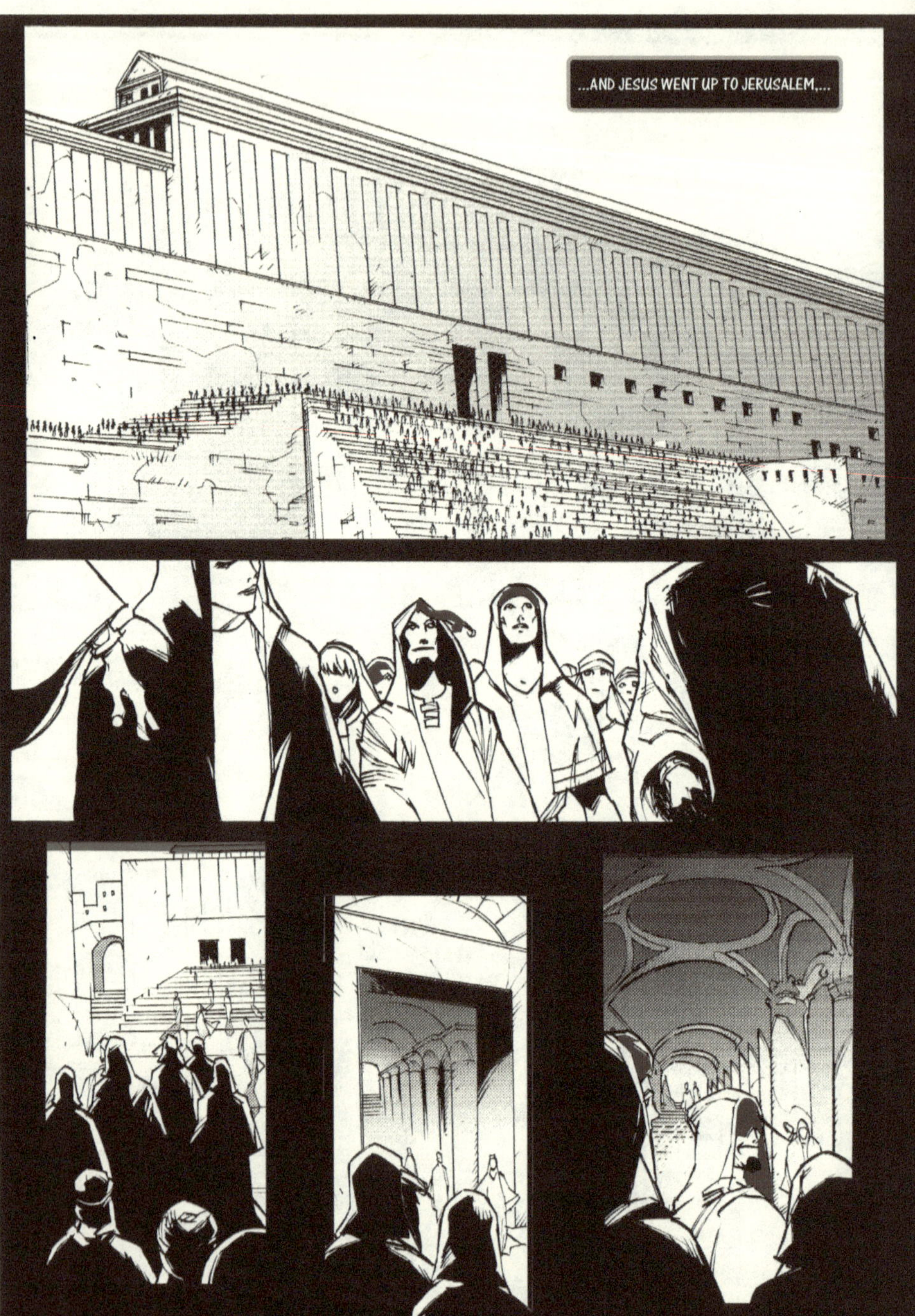
...AND JESUS WENT UP TO JERUSALEM,...

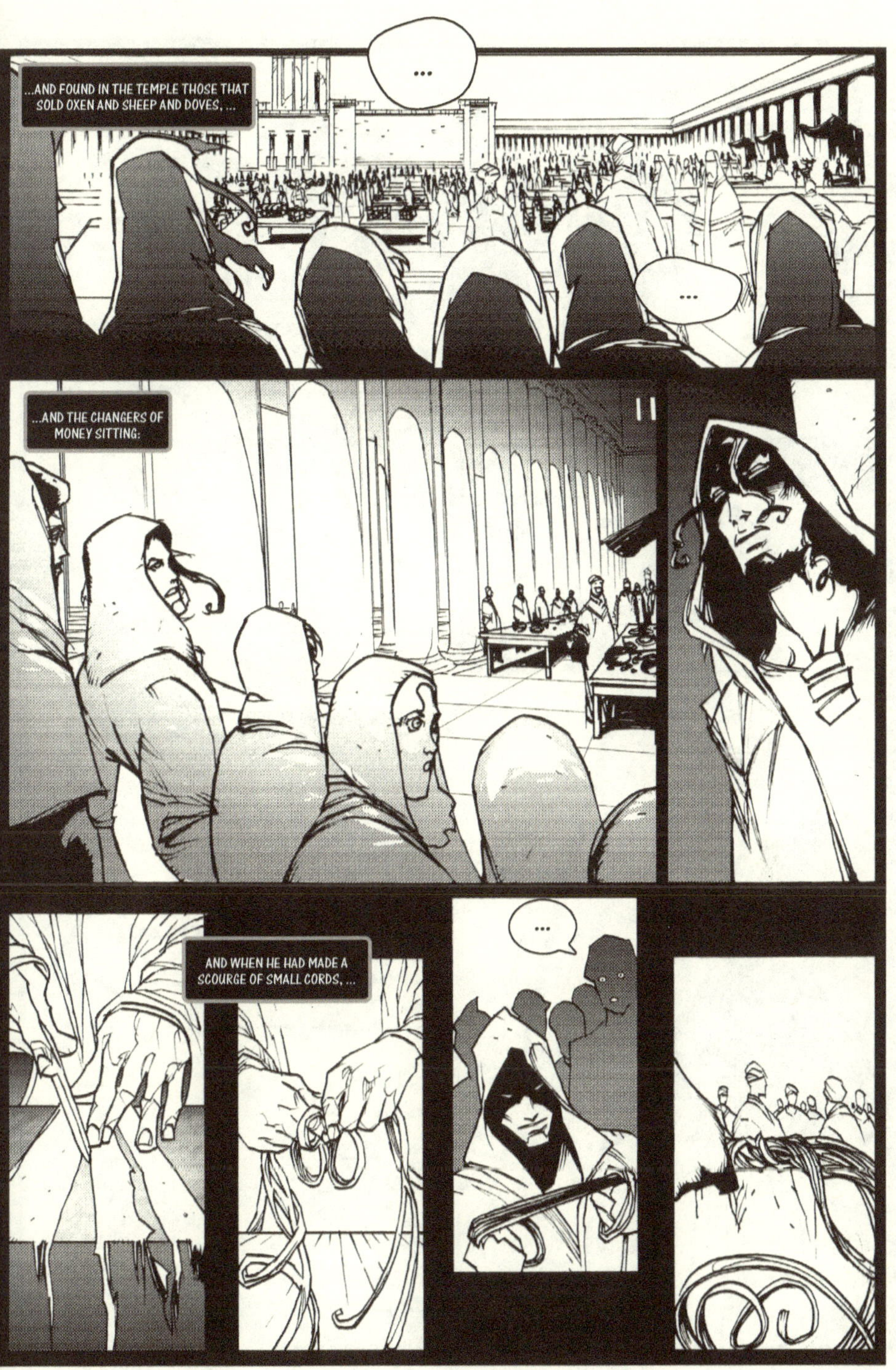
...AND FOUND IN THE TEMPLE THOSE THAT SOLD OXEN AND SHEEP AND DOVES, ...
...
...
...AND THE CHANGERS OF MONEY SITTING:
AND WHEN HE HAD MADE A SCOURGE OF SMALL CORDS, ...
...

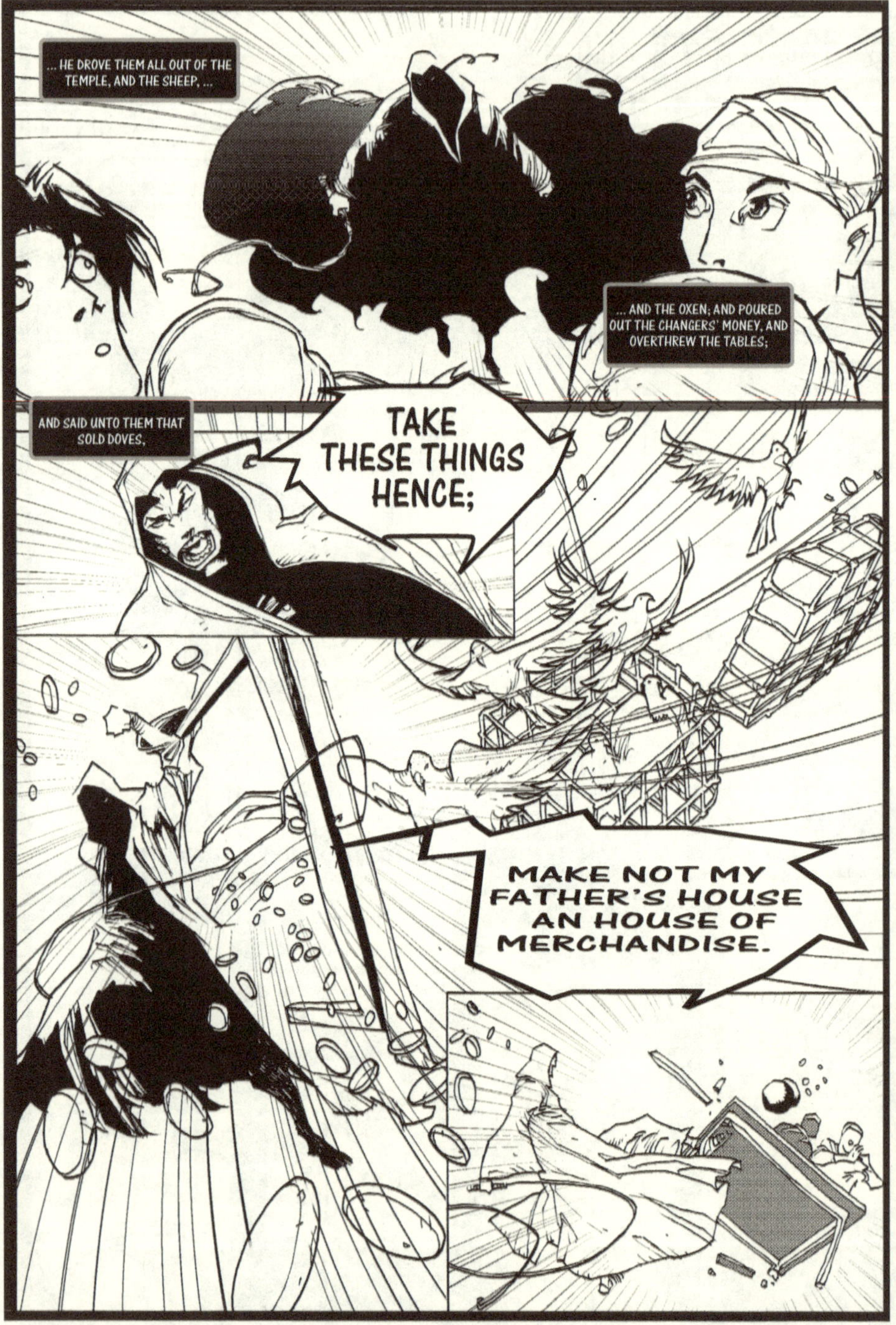
... HE DROVE THEM ALL OUT OF THE TEMPLE, AND THE SHEEP, ...
... AND THE OXEN; AND POURED OUT THE CHANGERS' MONEY, AND OVERTHREW THE TABLES;
AND SAID UNTO THEM THAT SOLD DOVES,
TAKE THESE THINGS HENCE;
MAKE NOT MY FATHER'S HOUSE AN HOUSE OF MERCHANDISE.

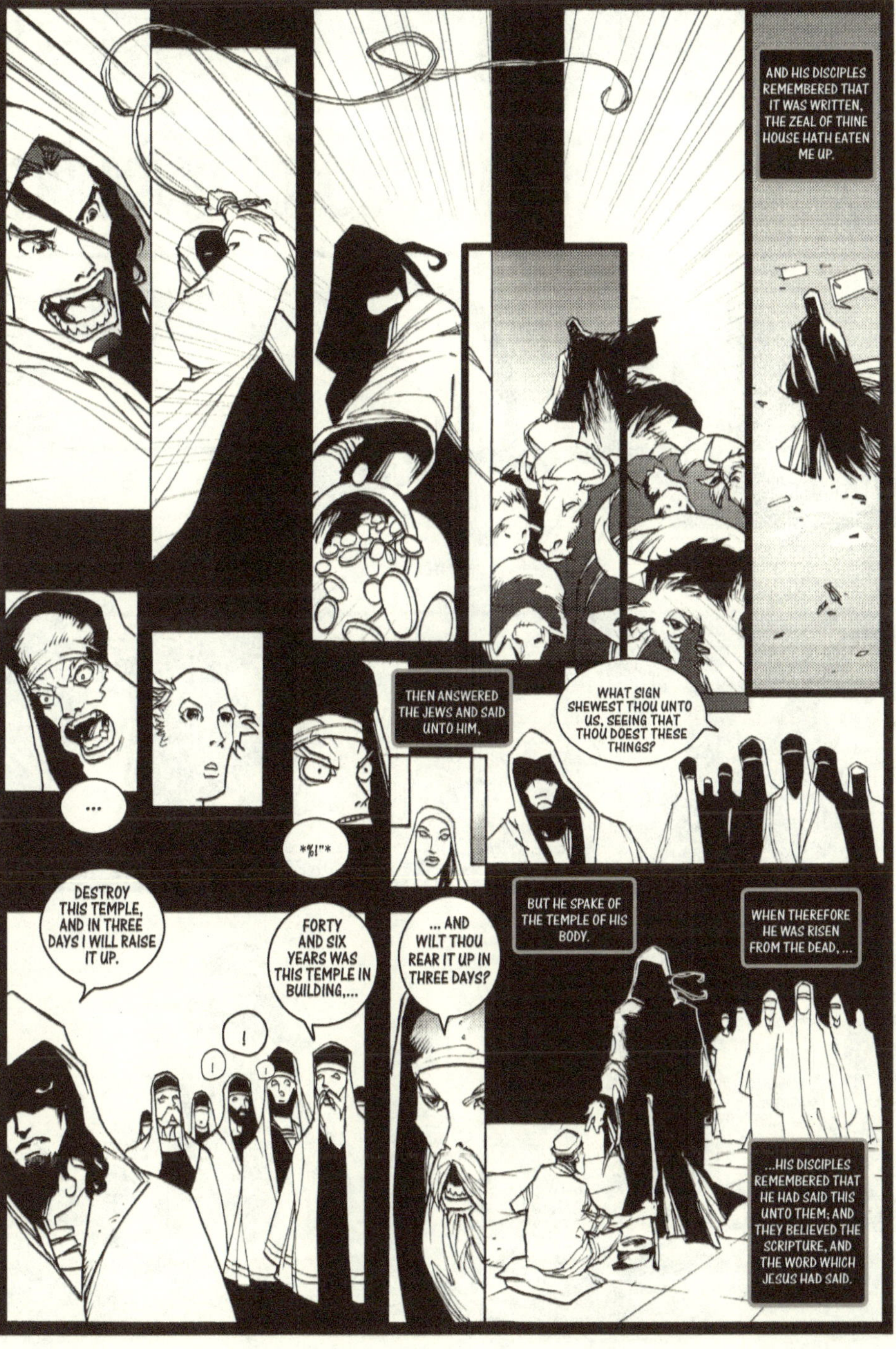
AND HIS DISCIPLES REMEMBERED THAT IT WAS WRITTEN, THE ZEAL OF THINE HOUSE HATH EATEN ME UP.
...
%!"
THEN ANSWERED THE JEWS AND SAID UNTO HIM,
WHAT SIGN SHEWEST THOU UNTO US, SEEING THAT THOU DOEST THESE THINGS?
DESTROY THIS TEMPLE, AND IN THREE DAYS I WILL RAISE IT UP.
!
!
!
FORTY AND SIX YEARS WAS THIS TEMPLE IN BUILDING,...
... AND WILT THOU REAR IT UP IN THREE DAYS?
BUT HE SPAKE OF THE TEMPLE OF HIS BODY.
WHEN THEREFORE HE WAS RISEN FROM THE DEAD, ...
...HIS DISCIPLES REMEMBERED THAT HE HAD SAID THIS UNTO THEM; AND THEY BELIEVED THE SCRIPTURE, AND THE WORD WHICH JESUS HAD SAID.

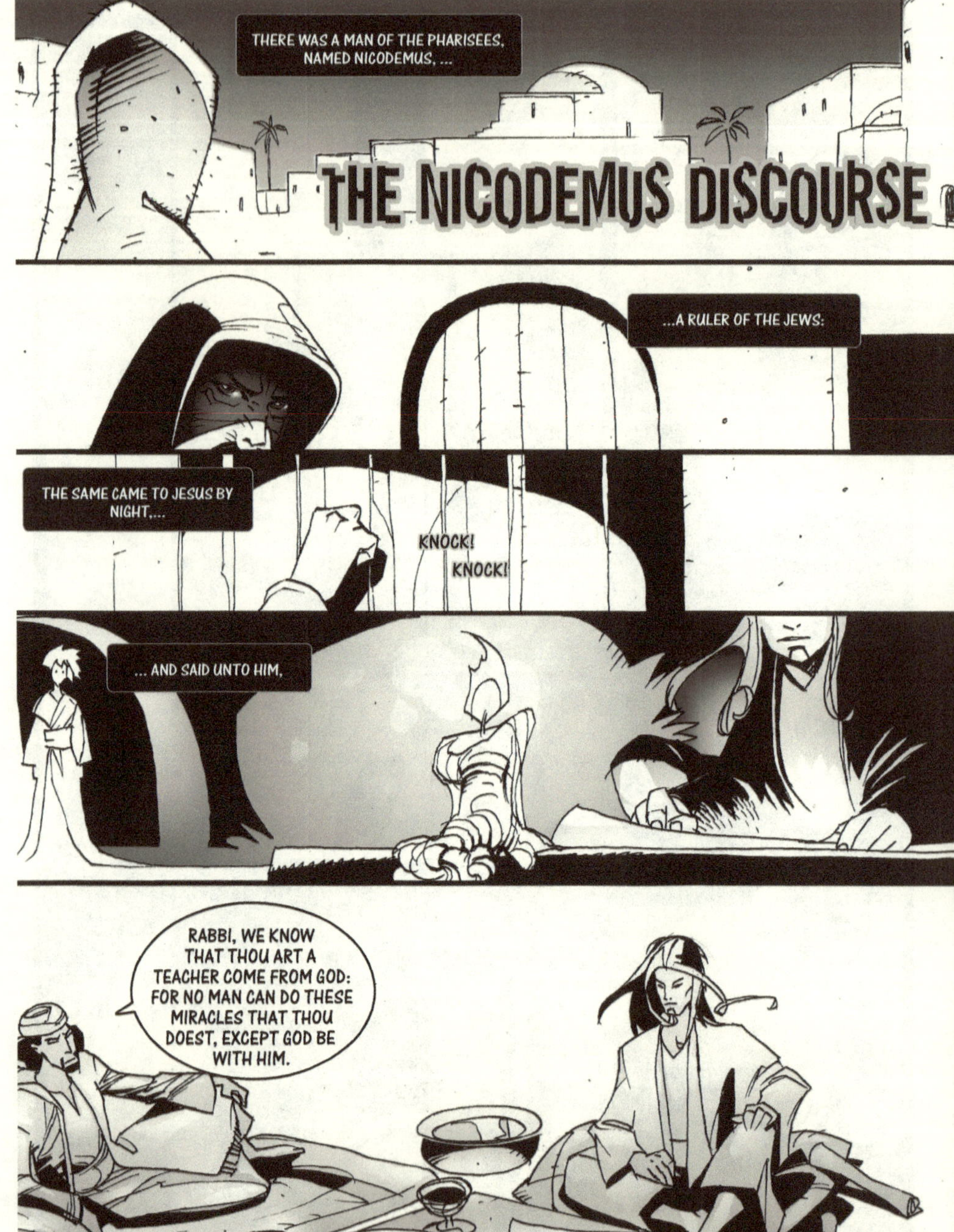
THERE WAS A MAN OF THE PHARISEES, NAMED NICODEMUS, ...
THE NICODEMUS DISCOURSE
...A RULER OF THE JEWS:
THE SAME CAME TO JESUS BY NIGHT,...
KNOCK!
KNOCK!
... AND SAID UNTO HIM,
RABBI, WE KNOW THAT THOU ART A TEACHER COME FROM GOD: FOR NO MAN CAN DO THESE MIRACLES THAT THOU DOEST, EXCEPT GOD BE WITH HIM.

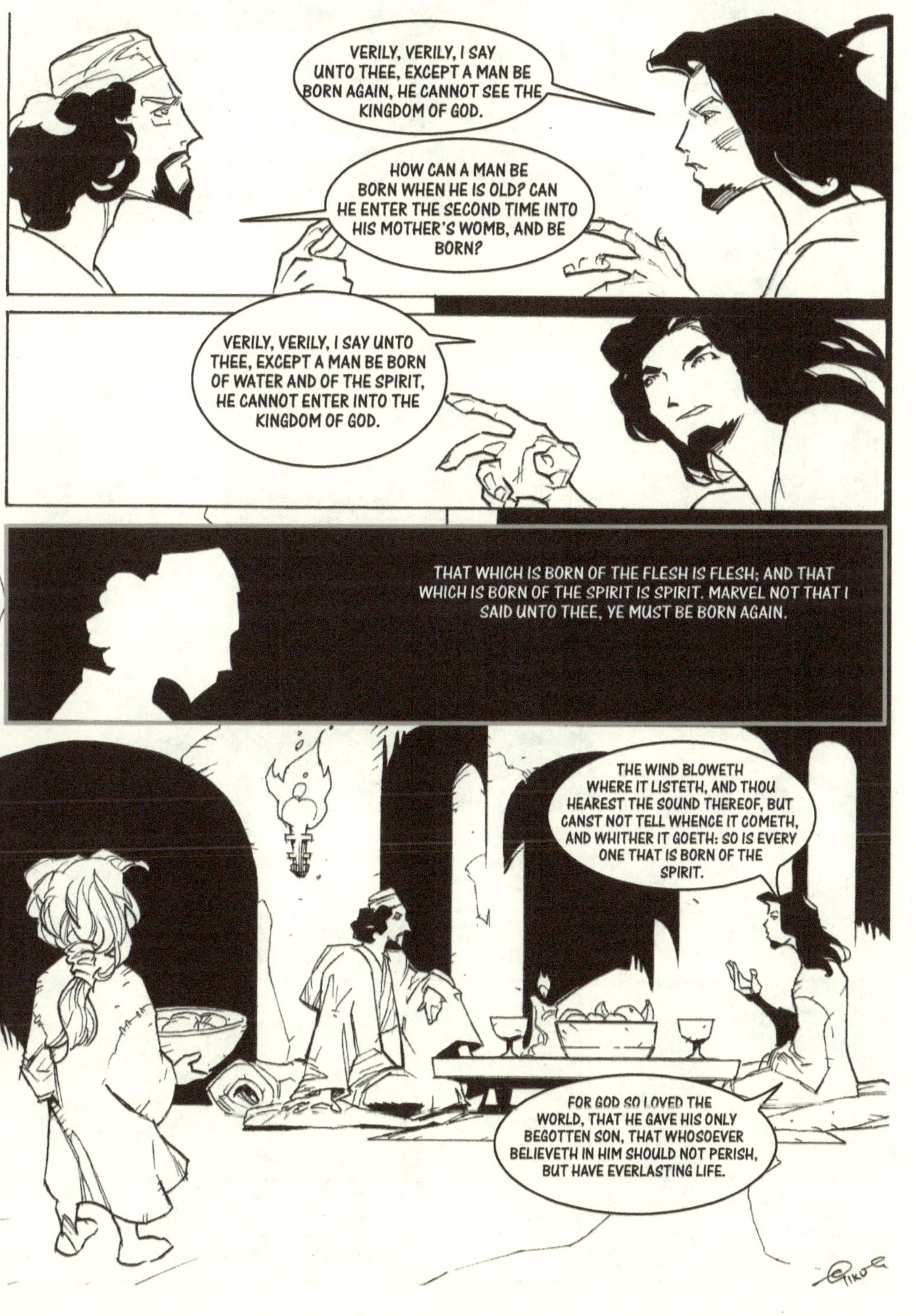
VERILY, VERILY, I SAY UNTO THEE, EXCEPT A MAN BE BORN AGAIN, HE CANNOT SEE THE KINGDOM OF GOD.
HOW CAN A MAN BE BORN WHEN HE IS OLD? CAN HE ENTER THE SECOND TIME INTO HIS MOTHER'S WOMB, AND BE BORN?
VERILY, VERILY, I SAY UNTO THEE, EXCEPT A MAN BE BORN OF WATER AND OF THE SPIRIT, HE CANNOT ENTER INTO THE KINGDOM OF GOD.
THAT WHICH IS BORN OF THE FLESH IS FLESH; AND THAT WHICH IS BORN OF THE SPIRIT IS SPIRIT. MARVEL NOT THAT I SAID UNTO THEE, YE MUST BE BORN AGAIN.
THE WIND BLOWETH WHERE IT LISTETH, AND THOU HEAREST THE SOUND THEREOF, BUT CANST NOT TELL WHENCE IT COMETH, AND WHITHER IT GOETH: SO IS EVERY ONE THAT IS BORN OF THE SPIRIT.
FOR GOD SO LOVED THE WORLD, THAT HE GAVE HIS ONLY BEGOTTEN SON, THAT WHOSOEVER BELIEVETH IN HIM SHOULD NOT PERISH, BUT HAVE EVERLASTING LIFE.

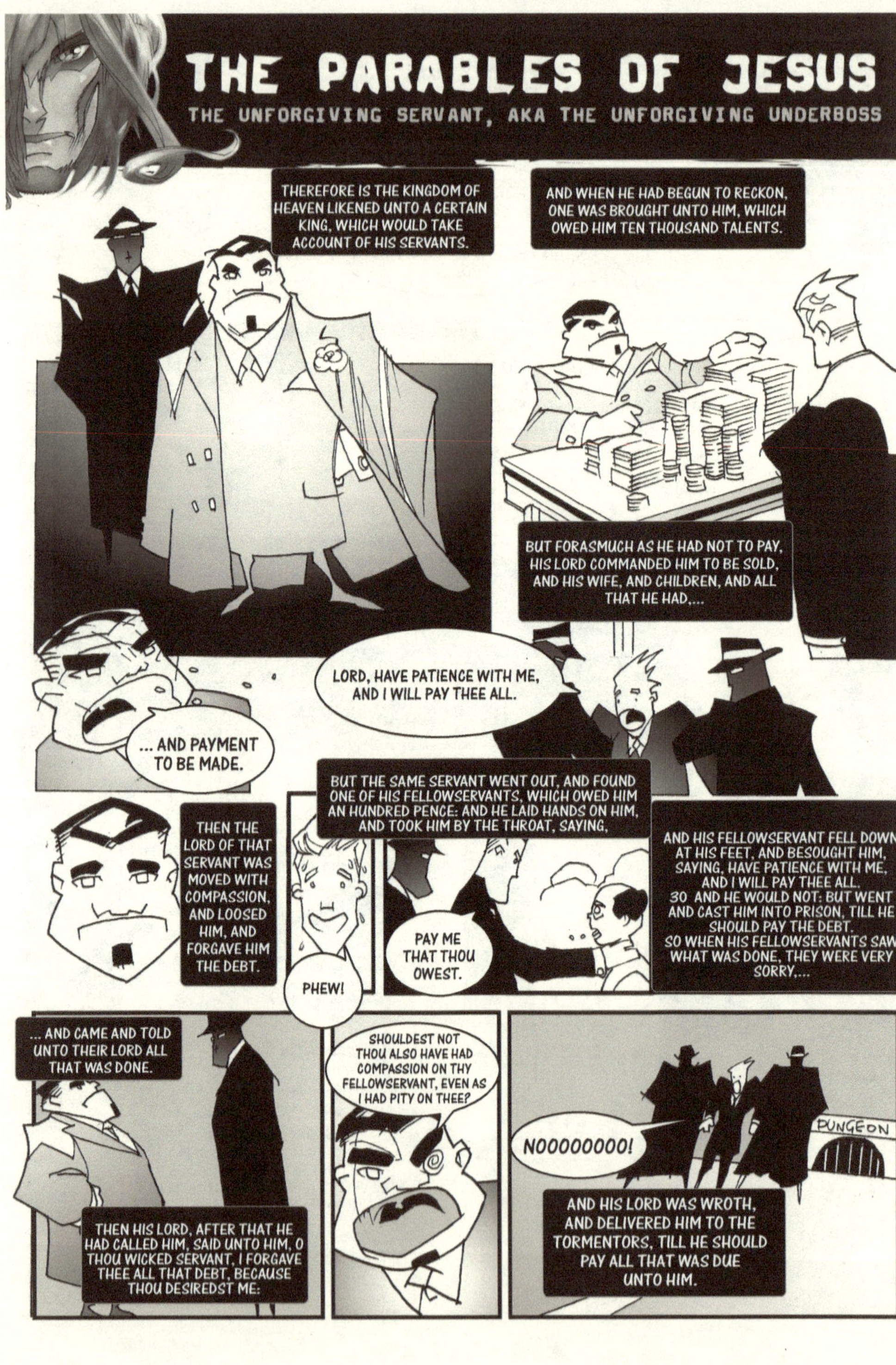
THE PARABLES OF JESUS
THE UNFORGIVING SERVANT, AKA THE UNFORGIVING UNDERBOSS
THEREFORE IS THE KINGDOM OF HEAVEN LIKENED UNTO A CERTAIN KING, WHICH WOULD TAKE ACCOUNT OF HIS SERVANTS.
AND WHEN HE HAD BEGUN TO RECKON, ONE WAS BROUGHT UNTO HIM, WHICH OWED HIM TEN THOUSAND TALENTS.
BUT FORASMUCH AS HE HAD NOT TO PAY, HIS LORD COMMANDED HIM TO BE SOLD, AND HIS WIFE, AND CHILDREN, AND ALL THAT HE HAD,...
... AND PAYMENT TO BE MADE.
LORD, HAVE PATIENCE WITH ME, AND I WILL PAY THEE ALL.
THEN THE LORD OF THAT SERVANT WAS MOVED WITH COMPASSION, AND LOOSED HIM, AND FORGAVE HIM THE DEBT.
PHEW!
BUT THE SAME SERVANT WENT OUT, AND FOUND ONE OF HIS FELLOWSERVANTS, WHICH OWED HIM AN HUNDRED PENCE: AND HE LAID HANDS ON HIM, AND TOOK HIM BY THE THROAT, SAYING,
PAY ME THAT THOU OWEST.
AND HIS FELLOWSERVANT FELL DOWN AT HIS FEET, AND BESOUGHT HIM, SAYING, HAVE PATIENCE WITH ME, AND I WILL PAY THEE ALL.
30 AND HE WOULD NOT: BUT WENT AND CAST HIM INTO PRISON, TILL HE SHOULD PAY THE DEBT.
SO WHEN HIS FELLOWSERVANTS SAW WHAT WAS DONE, THEY WERE VERY SORRY,...
... AND CAME AND TOLD UNTO THEIR LORD ALL THAT WAS DONE.
THEN HIS LORD, AFTER THAT HE HAD CALLED HIM, SAID UNTO HIM, O THOU WICKED SERVANT, I FORGAVE THEE ALL THAT DEBT, BECAUSE THOU DESIREDST ME:
SHOULDEST NOT THOU ALSO HAVE HAD COMPASSION ON THY FELLOWSERVANT, EVEN AS I HAD PITY ON THEE?
NOOOOOOOO!
DUNGEON
AND HIS LORD WAS WROTH, AND DELIVERED HIM TO THE TORMENTORS, TILL HE SHOULD PAY ALL THAT WAS DUE UNTO HIM.

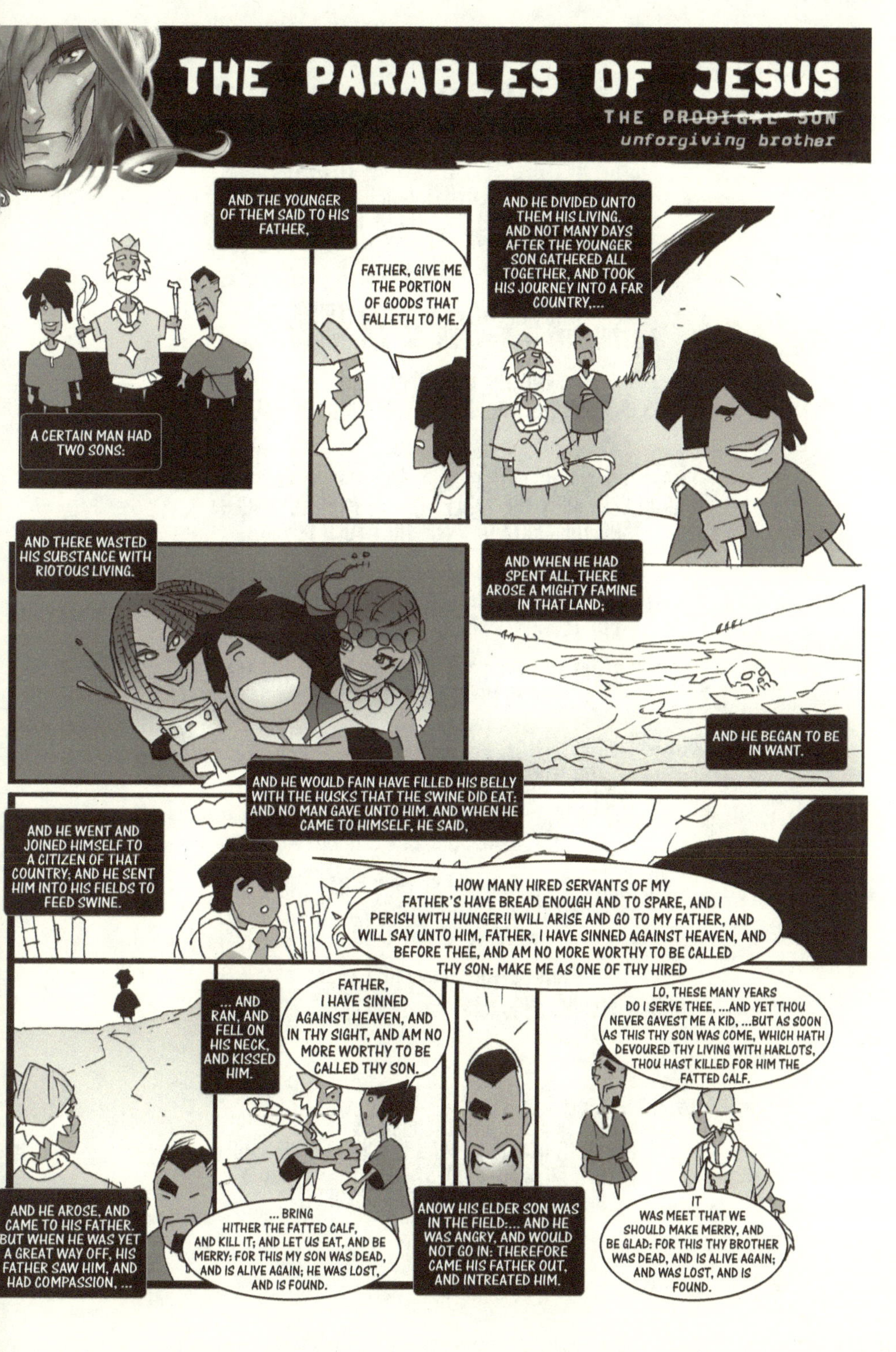
THE PARABLES OF JESUS
THE ~~PRODIGAL SON~~
unforgiving brother
A CERTAIN MAN HAD TWO SONS:
AND THE YOUNGER OF THEM SAID TO HIS FATHER,
FATHER, GIVE ME THE PORTION OF GOODS THAT FALLETH TO ME.
AND HE DIVIDED UNTO THEM HIS LIVING. AND NOT MANY DAYS AFTER THE YOUNGER SON GATHERED ALL TOGETHER, AND TOOK HIS JOURNEY INTO A FAR COUNTRY,...
AND THERE WASTED HIS SUBSTANCE WITH RIOTOUS LIVING.
AND WHEN HE HAD SPENT ALL, THERE AROSE A MIGHTY FAMINE IN THAT LAND;
AND HE BEGAN TO BE IN WANT.
AND HE WENT AND JOINED HIMSELF TO A CITIZEN OF THAT COUNTRY; AND HE SENT HIM INTO HIS FIELDS TO FEED SWINE.
AND HE WOULD FAIN HAVE FILLED HIS BELLY WITH THE HUSKS THAT THE SWINE DID EAT: AND NO MAN GAVE UNTO HIM. AND WHEN HE CAME TO HIMSELF, HE SAID,
HOW MANY HIRED SERVANTS OF MY FATHER'S HAVE BREAD ENOUGH AND TO SPARE, AND I PERISH WITH HUNGER!I WILL ARISE AND GO TO MY FATHER, AND WILL SAY UNTO HIM, FATHER, I HAVE SINNED AGAINST HEAVEN, AND BEFORE THEE, AND AM NO MORE WORTHY TO BE CALLED THY SON: MAKE ME AS ONE OF THY HIRED
AND HE AROSE, AND CAME TO HIS FATHER. BUT WHEN HE WAS YET A GREAT WAY OFF, HIS FATHER SAW HIM, AND HAD COMPASSION, ...
... AND RAN, AND FELL ON HIS NECK, AND KISSED HIM.
FATHER, I HAVE SINNED AGAINST HEAVEN, AND IN THY SIGHT, AND AM NO MORE WORTHY TO BE CALLED THY SON.
... BRING HITHER THE FATTED CALF, AND KILL IT; AND LET US EAT, AND BE MERRY: FOR THIS MY SON WAS DEAD, AND IS ALIVE AGAIN; HE WAS LOST, AND IS FOUND.
ANOW HIS ELDER SON WAS IN THE FIELD:... AND HE WAS ANGRY, AND WOULD NOT GO IN: THEREFORE CAME HIS FATHER OUT, AND INTREATED HIM.
LO, THESE MANY YEARS DO I SERVE THEE, ...AND YET THOU NEVER GAVEST ME A KID, ...BUT AS SOON AS THIS THY SON WAS COME, WHICH HATH DEVOURED THY LIVING WITH HARLOTS, THOU HAST KILLED FOR HIM THE FATTED CALF.
IT WAS MEET THAT WE SHOULD MAKE MERRY, AND BE GLAD: FOR THIS THY BROTHER WAS DEAD, AND IS ALIVE AGAIN; AND WAS LOST, AND IS FOUND.

AND THE MULTITUDES THAT WENT BEFORE
AND THAT FOLLOWED CRIED SAYING
HOSANNA TO THE SON OF DAVID
BLESSED IS HE THAT COMETH IN THE NAME OF THE LORD
HOSANNA IN THE HIGHEST

AND WHEN HE WAS COME INTO JERUSALEM
ALL THE CITY WAS MOVED SAYING WHO IS THIS

AND THE MULTITUDE SAID
THIS IS JESUS THE PROPHET OF NAZARETH OF GALILEE

AND JESUS WENT INTO THE TEMPLE OF GOD
AND CAST OUT ALL THEM THAT SOLD AND BOUGHT IN THE TEMPLE
AND OVERTHREW THE TABLES OF THE MONEYCHANGERS
AND THE SEATS OF THEM THAT SOLD DOVES

AND SAID UNTO THEM IT IS WRITTEN
MY HOUSE SHALL BE CALLED THE HOUSE OF PRAYER
BUT YE HAVE MADE IT A DEN OF THIEVES

AND THE BLIND AND THE LAME CAME TO HIM IN THE TEMPLE
AND HE HEALED THEM

AND WHEN THE CHIEF PRIESTS AND SCRIBES SAW
THE WONDERFUL THINGS THAT HE DID
AND THE CHILDREN CRYING IN THE TEMPLE
AND SAYING HOSANNA TO THE SON OF DAVID
THEY WERE SORE DISPLEASED

AND SAID UNTO HIM HEAREST THOU WHAT THESE SAY
AND JESUS SAITH UNTO THEM YEA
HAVE YE NEVER READ

OUT OF THE MOUTH OF BABES
AND SUCKLINGS THOU HAST PERFECTED PRAISE

AND WHEN HE WAS COME INTO THE TEMPLE
THE CHIEF PRIESTS AND THE ELDERS OF THE PEOPLE
CAME UNTO HIM AS HE WAS TEACHING AND SAID
BY WHAT AUTHORITY DOEST THOU THESE THINGS
AND WHO GAVE THEE THIS AUTHORITY

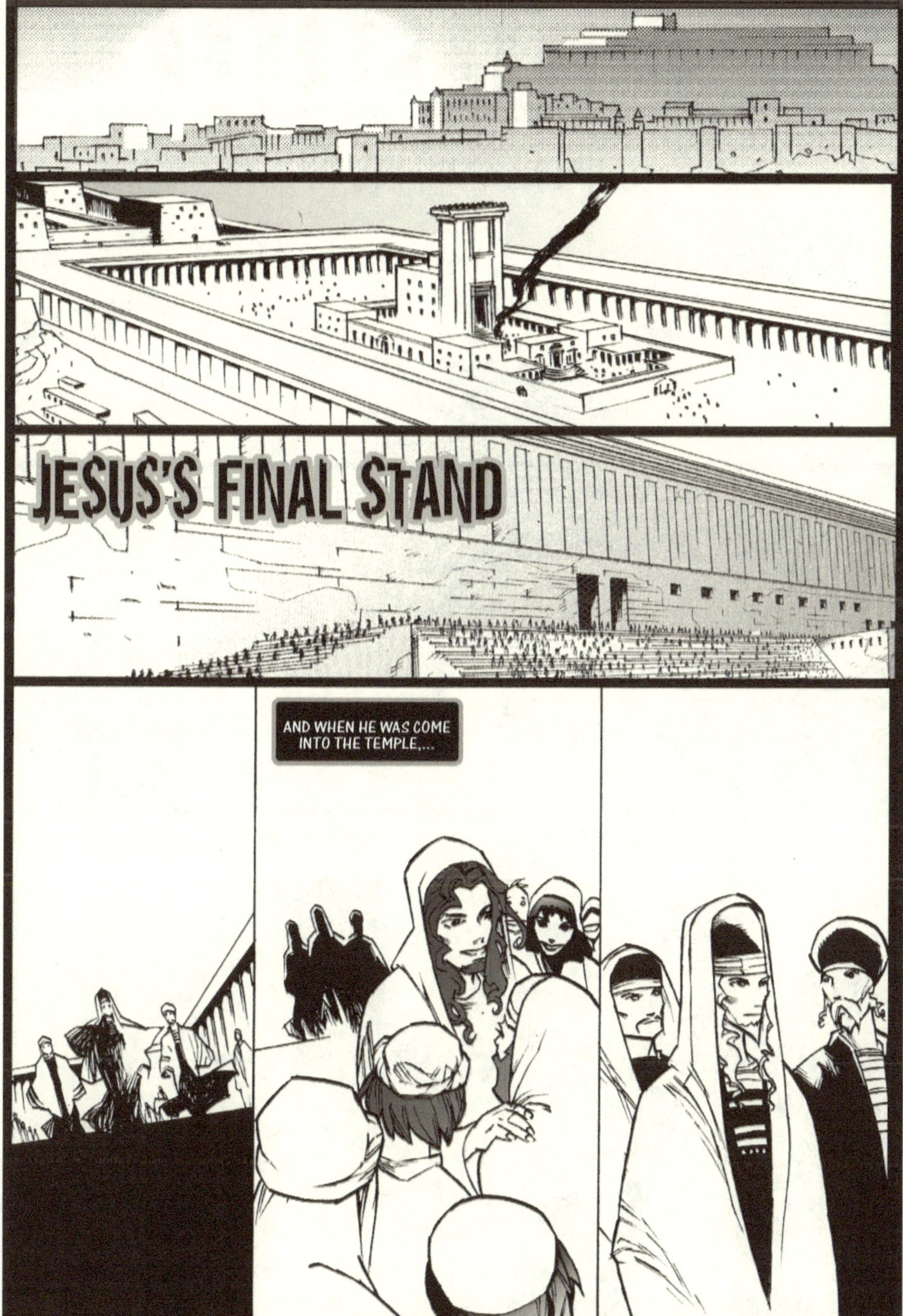
JESUS'S FINAL STAND
AND WHEN HE WAS COME INTO THE TEMPLE,...

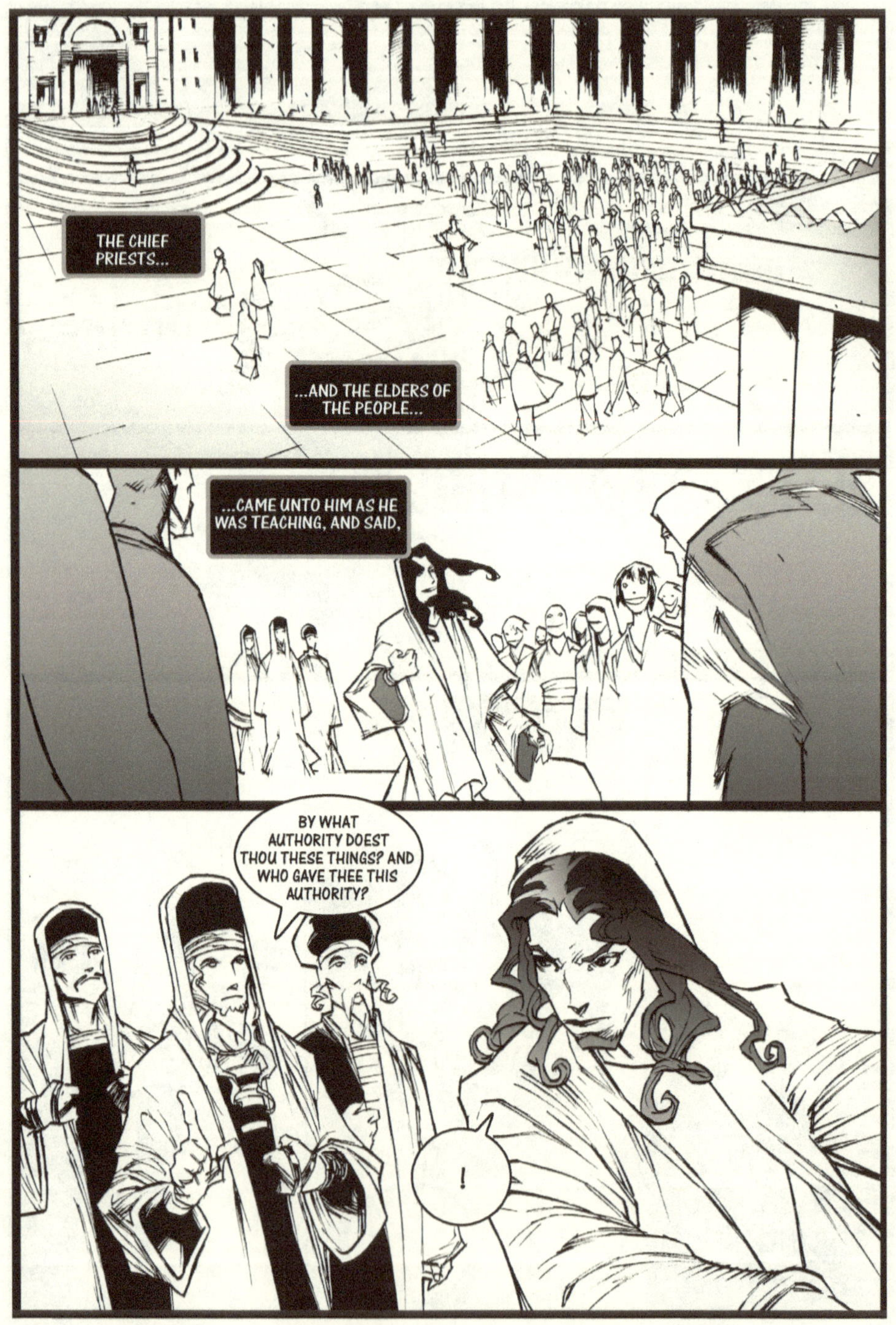
THE CHIEF PRIESTS...
...AND THE ELDERS OF THE PEOPLE...
...CAME UNTO HIM AS HE WAS TEACHING, AND SAID,
BY WHAT AUTHORITY DOEST THOU THESE THINGS? AND WHO GAVE THEE THIS AUTHORITY?
!

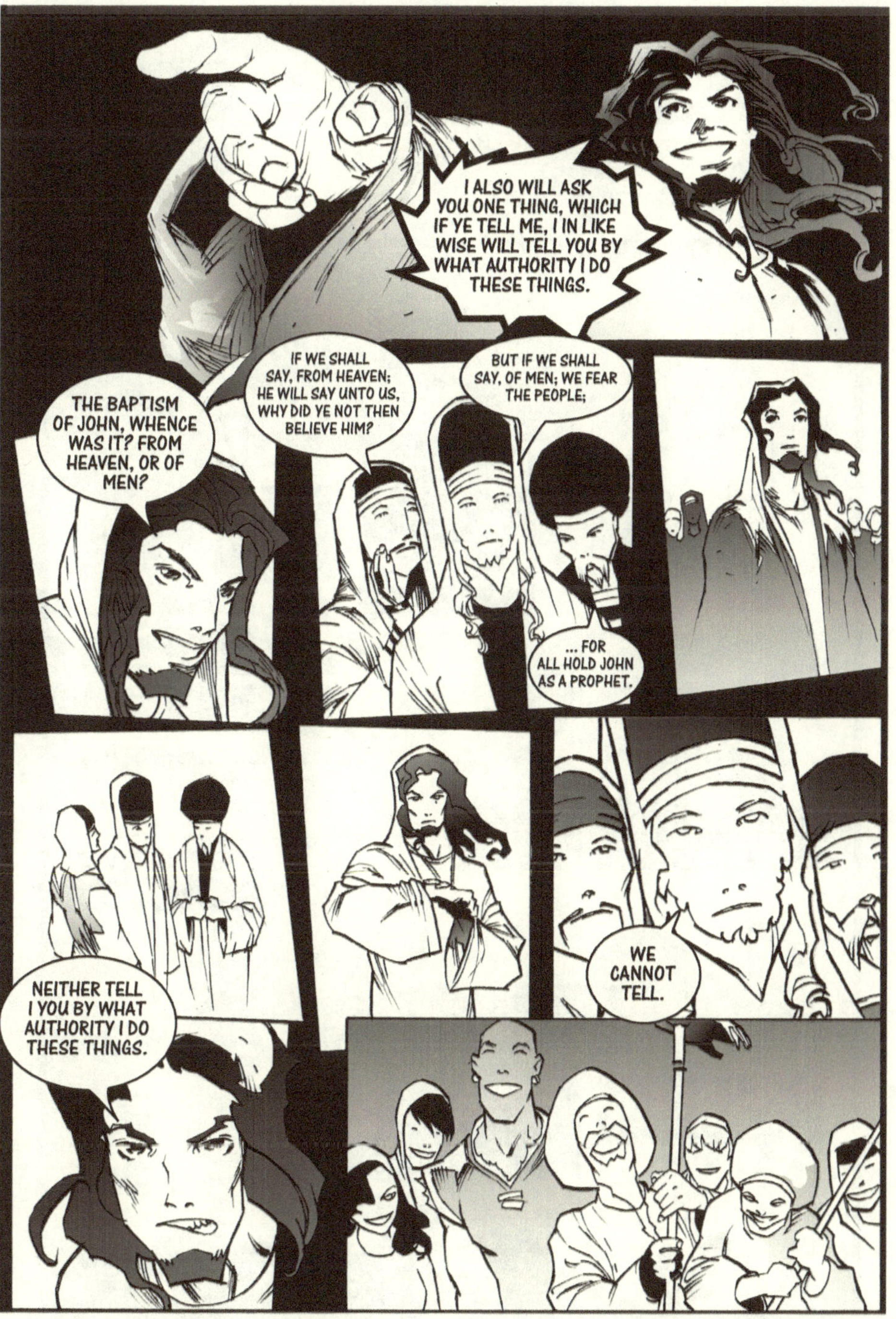
I ALSO WILL ASK YOU ONE THING, WHICH IF YE TELL ME, I IN LIKE WISE WILL TELL YOU BY WHAT AUTHORITY I DO THESE THINGS.
THE BAPTISM OF JOHN, WHENCE WAS IT? FROM HEAVEN, OR OF MEN?
IF WE SHALL SAY, FROM HEAVEN; HE WILL SAY UNTO US, WHY DID YE NOT THEN BELIEVE HIM?
BUT IF WE SHALL SAY, OF MEN; WE FEAR THE PEOPLE;
... FOR ALL HOLD JOHN AS A PROPHET.
WE CANNOT TELL.
NEITHER TELL I YOU BY WHAT AUTHORITY I DO THESE THINGS.

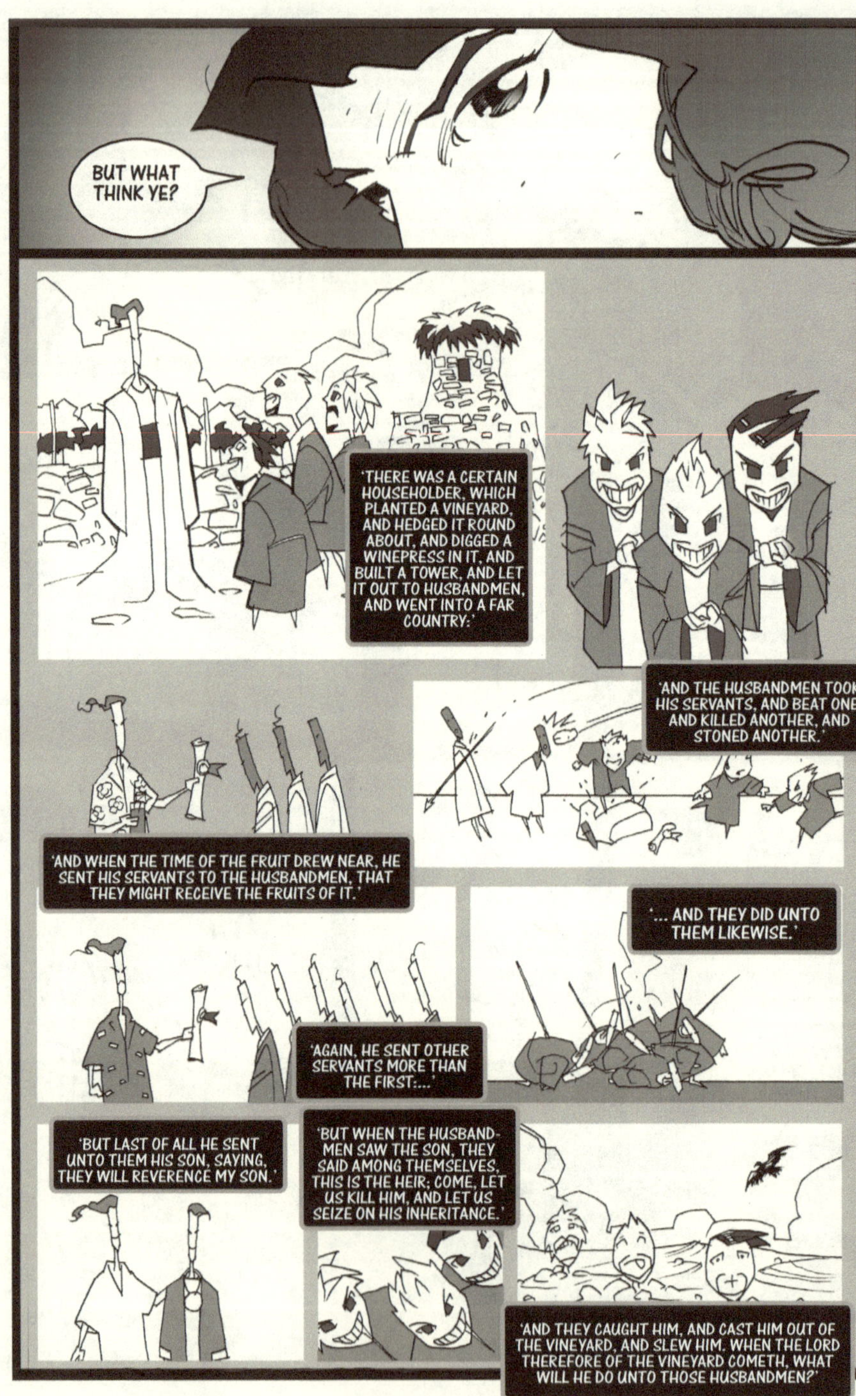
BUT WHAT THINK YE?
'THERE WAS A CERTAIN HOUSEHOLDER, WHICH PLANTED A VINEYARD, AND HEDGED IT ROUND ABOUT, AND DIGGED A WINEPRESS IN IT, AND BUILT A TOWER, AND LET IT OUT TO HUSBANDMEN, AND WENT INTO A FAR COUNTRY:'
'AND WHEN THE TIME OF THE FRUIT DREW NEAR, HE SENT HIS SERVANTS TO THE HUSBANDMEN, THAT THEY MIGHT RECEIVE THE FRUITS OF IT.'
'AND THE HUSBANDMEN TOOK HIS SERVANTS, AND BEAT ONE, AND KILLED ANOTHER, AND STONED ANOTHER.'
'AGAIN, HE SENT OTHER SERVANTS MORE THAN THE FIRST:...'
'... AND THEY DID UNTO THEM LIKEWISE.'
'BUT LAST OF ALL HE SENT UNTO THEM HIS SON, SAYING, THEY WILL REVERENCE MY SON.'
'BUT WHEN THE HUSBANDMEN SAW THE SON, THEY SAID AMONG THEMSELVES, THIS IS THE HEIR; COME, LET US KILL HIM, AND LET US SEIZE ON HIS INHERITANCE.'
'AND THEY CAUGHT HIM, AND CAST HIM OUT OF THE VINEYARD, AND SLEW HIM. WHEN THE LORD THEREFORE OF THE VINEYARD COMETH, WHAT WILL HE DO UNTO THOSE HUSBANDMEN?'

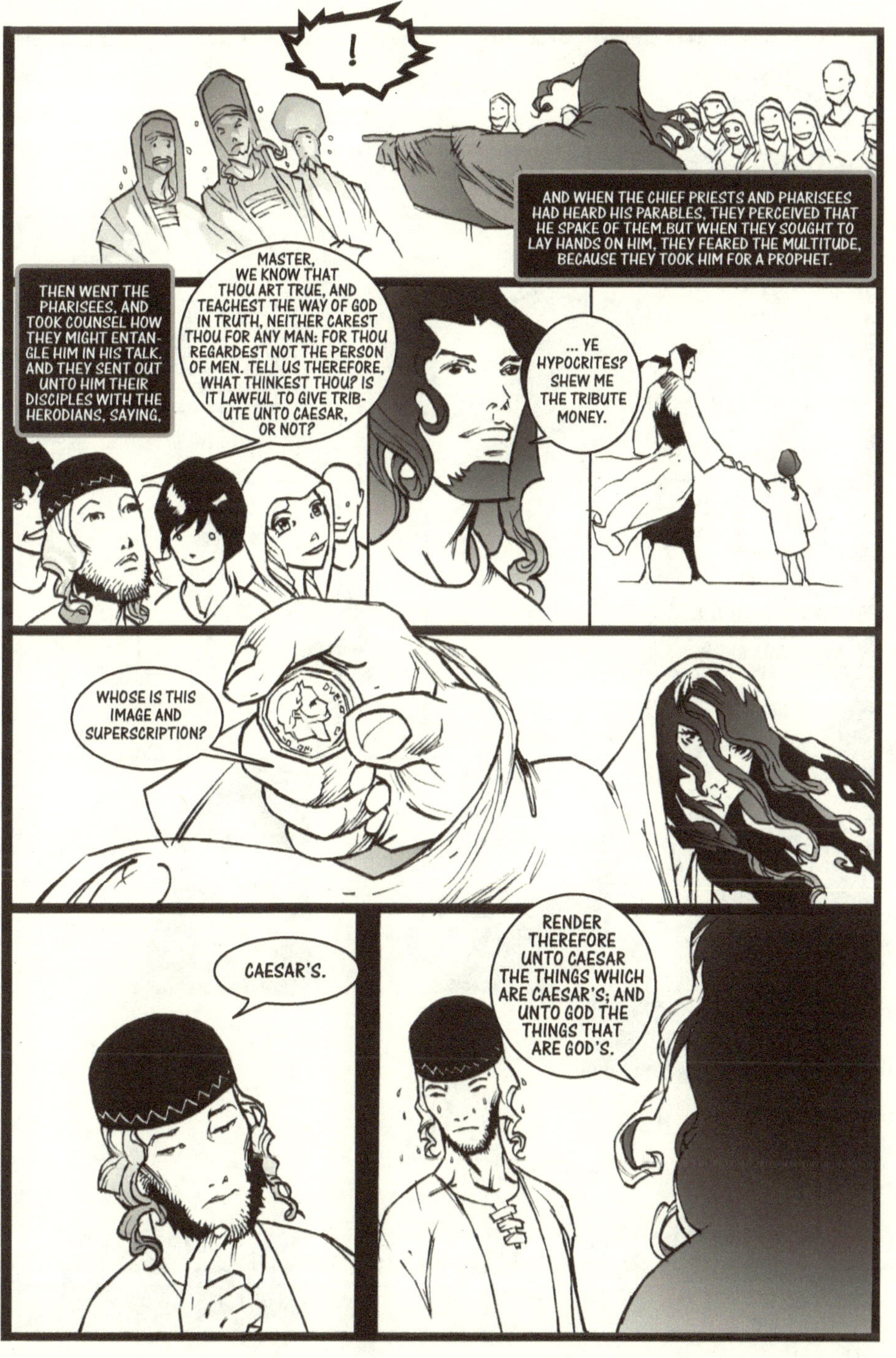
!
AND WHEN THE CHIEF PRIESTS AND PHARISEES HAD HEARD HIS PARABLES, THEY PERCEIVED THAT HE SPAKE OF THEM.BUT WHEN THEY SOUGHT TO LAY HANDS ON HIM, THEY FEARED THE MULTITUDE, BECAUSE THEY TOOK HIM FOR A PROPHET.
THEN WENT THE PHARISEES, AND TOOK COUNSEL HOW THEY MIGHT ENTANGLE HIM IN HIS TALK. AND THEY SENT OUT UNTO HIM THEIR DISCIPLES WITH THE HERODIANS, SAYING,
MASTER, WE KNOW THAT THOU ART TRUE, AND TEACHEST THE WAY OF GOD IN TRUTH, NEITHER CAREST THOU FOR ANY MAN: FOR THOU REGARDEST NOT THE PERSON OF MEN. TELL US THEREFORE, WHAT THINKEST THOU? IS IT LAWFUL TO GIVE TRIBUTE UNTO CAESAR, OR NOT?
... YE HYPOCRITES? SHEW ME THE TRIBUTE MONEY.
WHOSE IS THIS IMAGE AND SUPERSCRIPTION?
CAESAR'S.
RENDER THEREFORE UNTO CAESAR THE THINGS WHICH ARE CAESAR'S; AND UNTO GOD THE THINGS THAT ARE GOD'S.

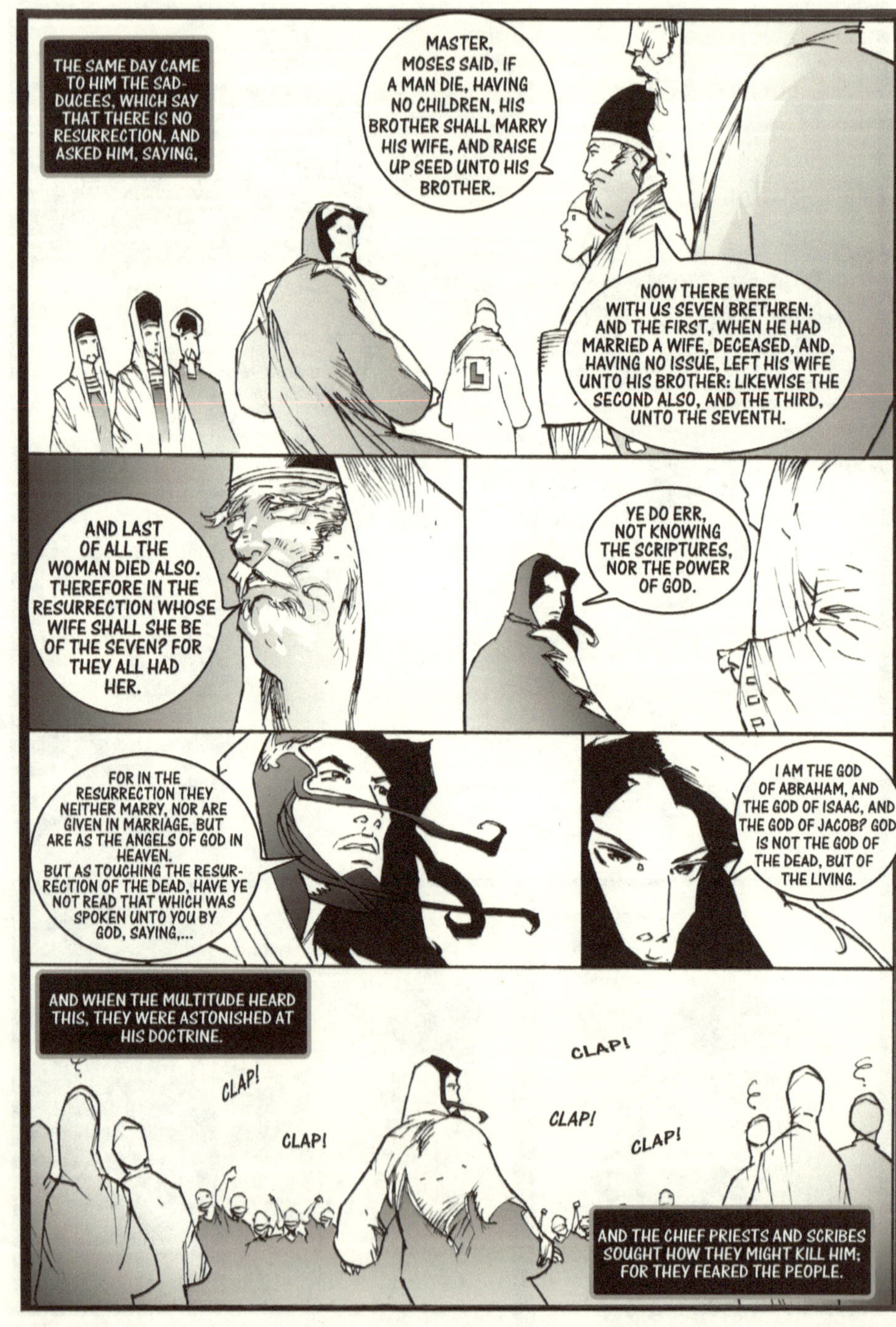
THE SAME DAY CAME TO HIM THE SAD-DUCEES, WHICH SAY THAT THERE IS NO RESURRECTION, AND ASKED HIM, SAYING,
MASTER, MOSES SAID, IF A MAN DIE, HAVING NO CHILDREN, HIS BROTHER SHALL MARRY HIS WIFE, AND RAISE UP SEED UNTO HIS BROTHER.
NOW THERE WERE WITH US SEVEN BRETHREN: AND THE FIRST, WHEN HE HAD MARRIED A WIFE, DECEASED, AND, HAVING NO ISSUE, LEFT HIS WIFE UNTO HIS BROTHER: LIKEWISE THE SECOND ALSO, AND THE THIRD, UNTO THE SEVENTH.
AND LAST OF ALL THE WOMAN DIED ALSO. THEREFORE IN THE RESURRECTION WHOSE WIFE SHALL SHE BE OF THE SEVEN? FOR THEY ALL HAD HER.
YE DO ERR, NOT KNOWING THE SCRIPTURES, NOR THE POWER OF GOD.
FOR IN THE RESURRECTION THEY NEITHER MARRY, NOR ARE GIVEN IN MARRIAGE, BUT ARE AS THE ANGELS OF GOD IN HEAVEN. BUT AS TOUCHING THE RESUR-RECTION OF THE DEAD, HAVE YE NOT READ THAT WHICH WAS SPOKEN UNTO YOU BY GOD, SAYING,...
I AM THE GOD OF ABRAHAM, AND THE GOD OF ISAAC, AND THE GOD OF JACOB? GOD IS NOT THE GOD OF THE DEAD, BUT OF THE LIVING.
AND WHEN THE MULTITUDE HEARD THIS, THEY WERE ASTONISHED AT HIS DOCTRINE.
CLAP!
CLAP!
CLAP!
CLAP!
CLAP!
AND THE CHIEF PRIESTS AND SCRIBES SOUGHT HOW THEY MIGHT KILL HIM; FOR THEY FEARED THE PEOPLE.

AND IT CAME TO PASS WHEN JESUS HAD FINISHED ALL THESE SAYINGS
HE SAID UNTO HIS DISCIPLES
YE KNOW THAT AFTER TWO DAYS IS THE FEAST OF THE PASSOVER
AND THE SON OF MAN IS BETRAYED TO BE CRUCIFIED
THEN ASSEMBLED TOGETHER THE CHIEF PRIESTS AND THE SCRIBES
AND THE ELDERS OF THE PEOPLE UNTO THE PALACE OF
THE HIGH PRIEST WHO WAS CALLED CAIAPHAS
AND CONSULTED THAT THEY MIGHT TAKE JESUS
BY SUBTILTY AND KILL HIM
BUT THEY SAID NOT ON THE FEAST DAY
LEST THERE BE AN UPROAR AMONG THE PEOPLE
NOW WHEN JESUS WAS IN BETHANY IN THE HOUSE OF SIMON THE LEPER
THERE CAME UNTO HIM A WOMAN HAVING AN ALABASTER BOX
OF VERY PRECIOUS OINTMENT AND POURED IT
ON HIS HEAD AS HE SAT AT MEAT
BUT WHEN HIS DISCIPLES SAW IT THEY HAD INDIGNATION
SAYING TO WHAT PURPOSE IS THIS WASTE
FOR THIS OINTMENT MIGHT HAVE BEEN SOLD FOR MUCH AND GIVEN TO THE POOR
WHEN JESUS UNDERSTOOD IT HE SAID UNTO THEM
WHY TROUBLE YE THE WOMAN FOR SHE
HATH WROUGHT A GOOD WORK UPON ME
FOR YE HAVE THE POOR ALWAYS WITH YOU
BUT ME YE HAVE NOT ALWAYS
FOR IN THAT SHE HATH POURED THIS OINTMENT ON MY BODY
SHE DID IT FOR MY BURIAL
VERILY I SAY UNTO YOU WHERESOEVER
THIS GOSPEL SHALL BE PREACHED IN THE WHOLE WORLD
THERE SHALL ALSO THIS THAT THIS WOMAN HATH DONE
BE TOLD FOR A MEMORIAL OF HER
THEN ONE OF THE TWELVE CALLED JUDAS ISCARIOT
WENT UNTO THE CHIEF PRIESTS
AND SAID UNTO THEM WHAT WILL YE GIVE ME AND I WILL DELIVER HIM UNTO YOU
AND THEY COVENANTED WITH HIM FOR THIRTY PIECES OF SILVER
AND FROM THAT TIME HE SOUGHT OPPORTUNITY TO BETRAY HIM

NOW THE FIRST DAY OF THE FEAST OF UNLEAVENED BREAD
THE DISCIPLES CAME TO JESUS SAYING UNTO HIM
WHERE WILT THOU THAT WE PREPARE FOR THEE TO EAT THE PASSOVER
AND HE SAID GO INTO THE CITY TO SUCH A MAN
AND SAY UNTO HIM THE MASTER SAITH MY TIME IS AT HAND
I WILL KEEP THE PASSOVER AT THY HOUSE WITH MY DISCIPLES
AND THE DISCIPLES DID AS JESUS HAD APPOINTED THEM
AND THEY MADE READY THE PASSOVER

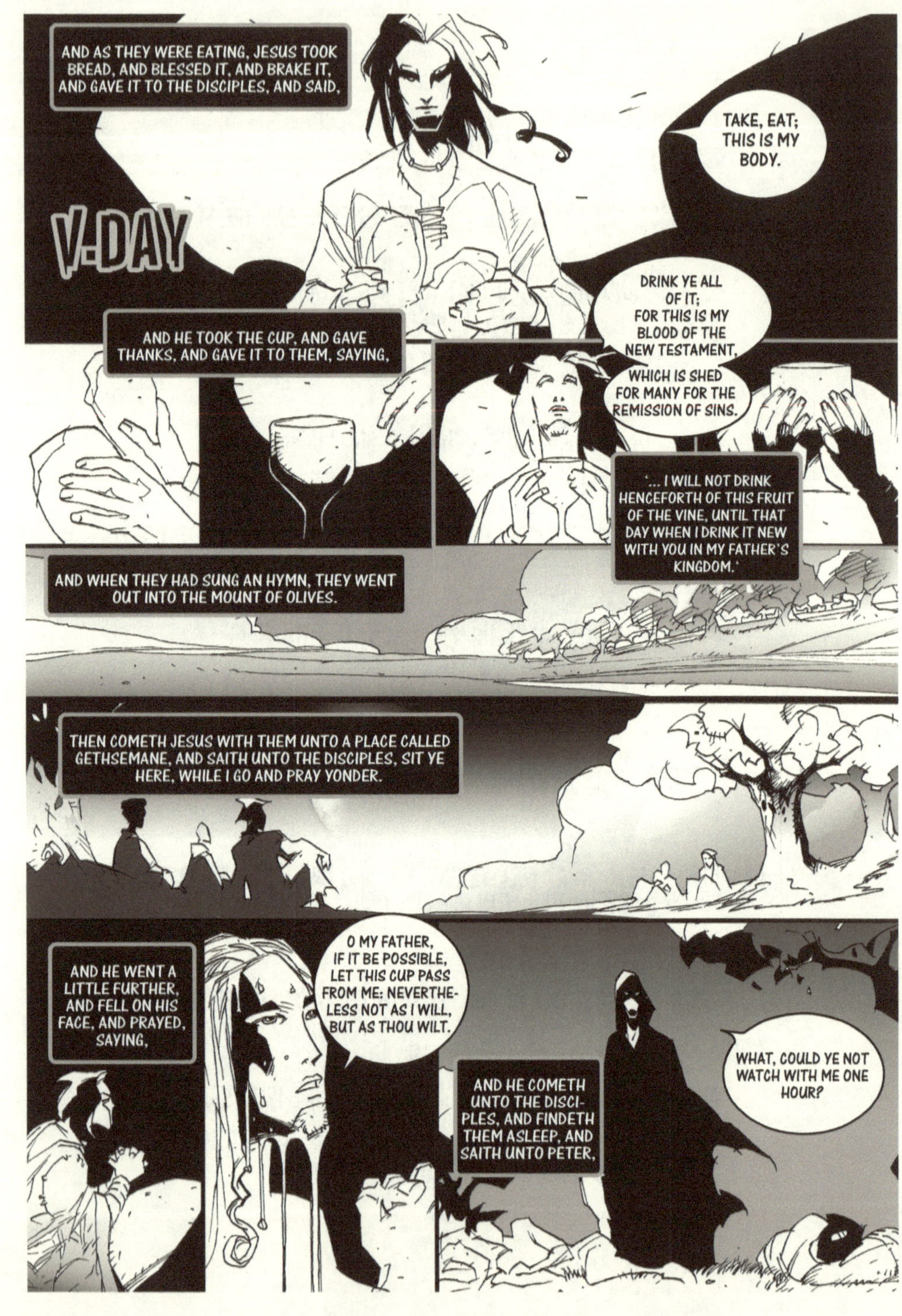

AND AS THEY WERE EATING, JESUS TOOK BREAD, AND BLESSED IT, AND BRAKE IT, AND GAVE IT TO THE DISCIPLES, AND SAID,
TAKE, EAT; THIS IS MY BODY.
V-DAY
AND HE TOOK THE CUP, AND GAVE THANKS, AND GAVE IT TO THEM, SAYING,
DRINK YE ALL OF IT; FOR THIS IS MY BLOOD OF THE NEW TESTAMENT,
WHICH IS SHED FOR MANY FOR THE REMISSION OF SINS.
'... I WILL NOT DRINK HENCEFORTH OF THIS FRUIT OF THE VINE, UNTIL THAT DAY WHEN I DRINK IT NEW WITH YOU IN MY FATHER'S KINGDOM.'
AND WHEN THEY HAD SUNG AN HYMN, THEY WENT OUT INTO THE MOUNT OF OLIVES.
THEN COMETH JESUS WITH THEM UNTO A PLACE CALLED GETHSEMANE, AND SAITH UNTO THE DISCIPLES, SIT YE HERE, WHILE I GO AND PRAY YONDER.
AND HE WENT A LITTLE FURTHER, AND FELL ON HIS FACE, AND PRAYED, SAYING,
O MY FATHER, IF IT BE POSSIBLE, LET THIS CUP PASS FROM ME: NEVERTHELESS NOT AS I WILL, BUT AS THOU WILT.
AND HE COMETH UNTO THE DISCIPLES, AND FINDETH THEM ASLEEP, AND SAITH UNTO PETER,
WHAT, COULD YE NOT WATCH WITH ME ONE HOUR?

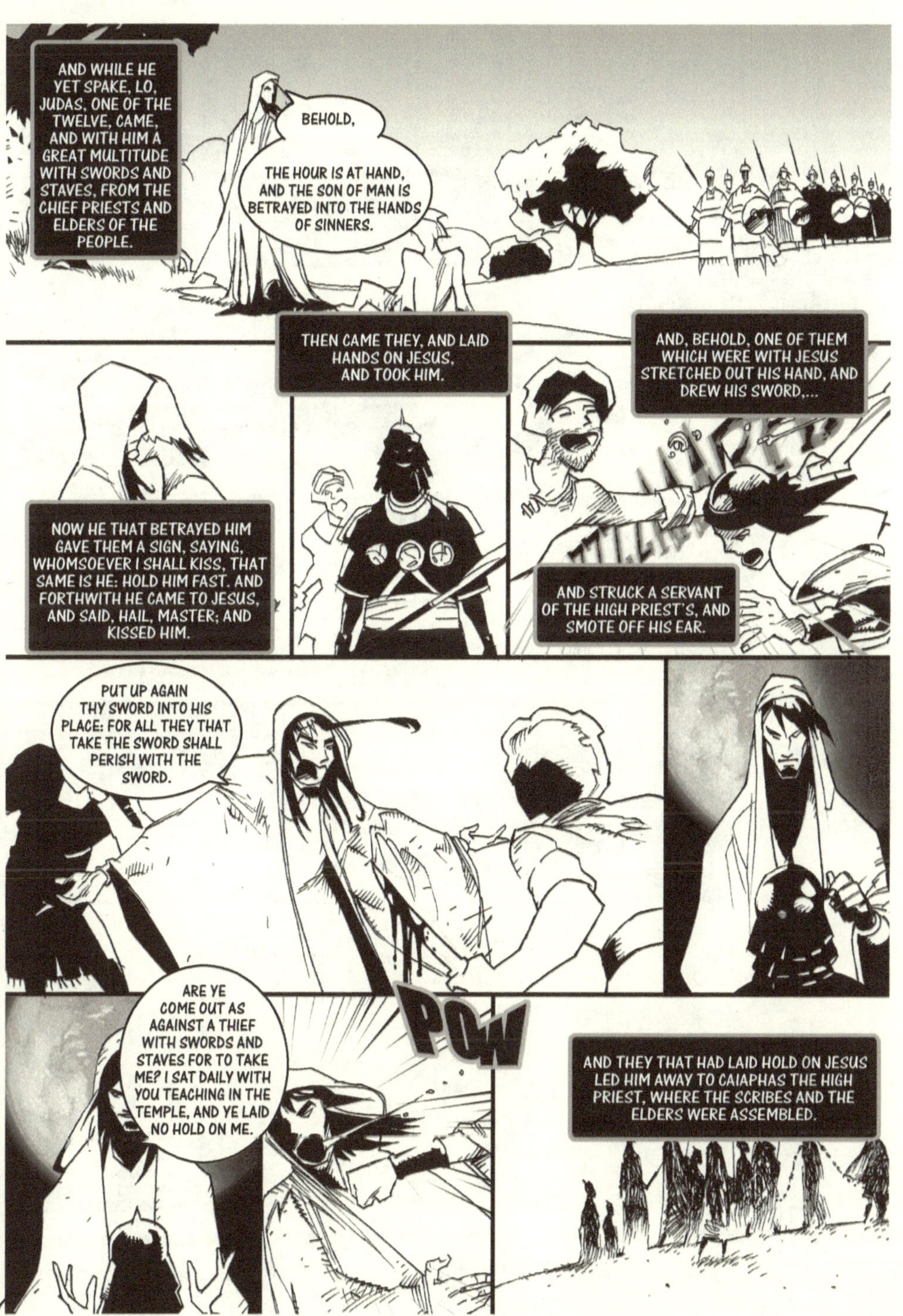
AND WHILE HE YET SPAKE, LO, JUDAS, ONE OF THE TWELVE, CAME, AND WITH HIM A GREAT MULTITUDE WITH SWORDS AND STAVES, FROM THE CHIEF PRIESTS AND ELDERS OF THE PEOPLE.
BEHOLD,
THE HOUR IS AT HAND, AND THE SON OF MAN IS BETRAYED INTO THE HANDS OF SINNERS.
NOW HE THAT BETRAYED HIM GAVE THEM A SIGN, SAYING, WHOMSOEVER I SHALL KISS, THAT SAME IS HE: HOLD HIM FAST. AND FORTHWITH HE CAME TO JESUS, AND SAID, HAIL, MASTER; AND KISSED HIM.
THEN CAME THEY, AND LAID HANDS ON JESUS, AND TOOK HIM.
AND, BEHOLD, ONE OF THEM WHICH WERE WITH JESUS STRETCHED OUT HIS HAND, AND DREW HIS SWORD,...
AND STRUCK A SERVANT OF THE HIGH PRIEST'S, AND SMOTE OFF HIS EAR.
PUT UP AGAIN THY SWORD INTO HIS PLACE: FOR ALL THEY THAT TAKE THE SWORD SHALL PERISH WITH THE SWORD.
ARE YE COME OUT AS AGAINST A THIEF WITH SWORDS AND STAVES FOR TO TAKE ME? I SAT DAILY WITH YOU TEACHING IN THE TEMPLE, AND YE LAID NO HOLD ON ME.
POW
AND THEY THAT HAD LAID HOLD ON JESUS LED HIM AWAY TO CAIAPHAS THE HIGH PRIEST, WHERE THE SCRIBES AND THE ELDERS WERE ASSEMBLED.

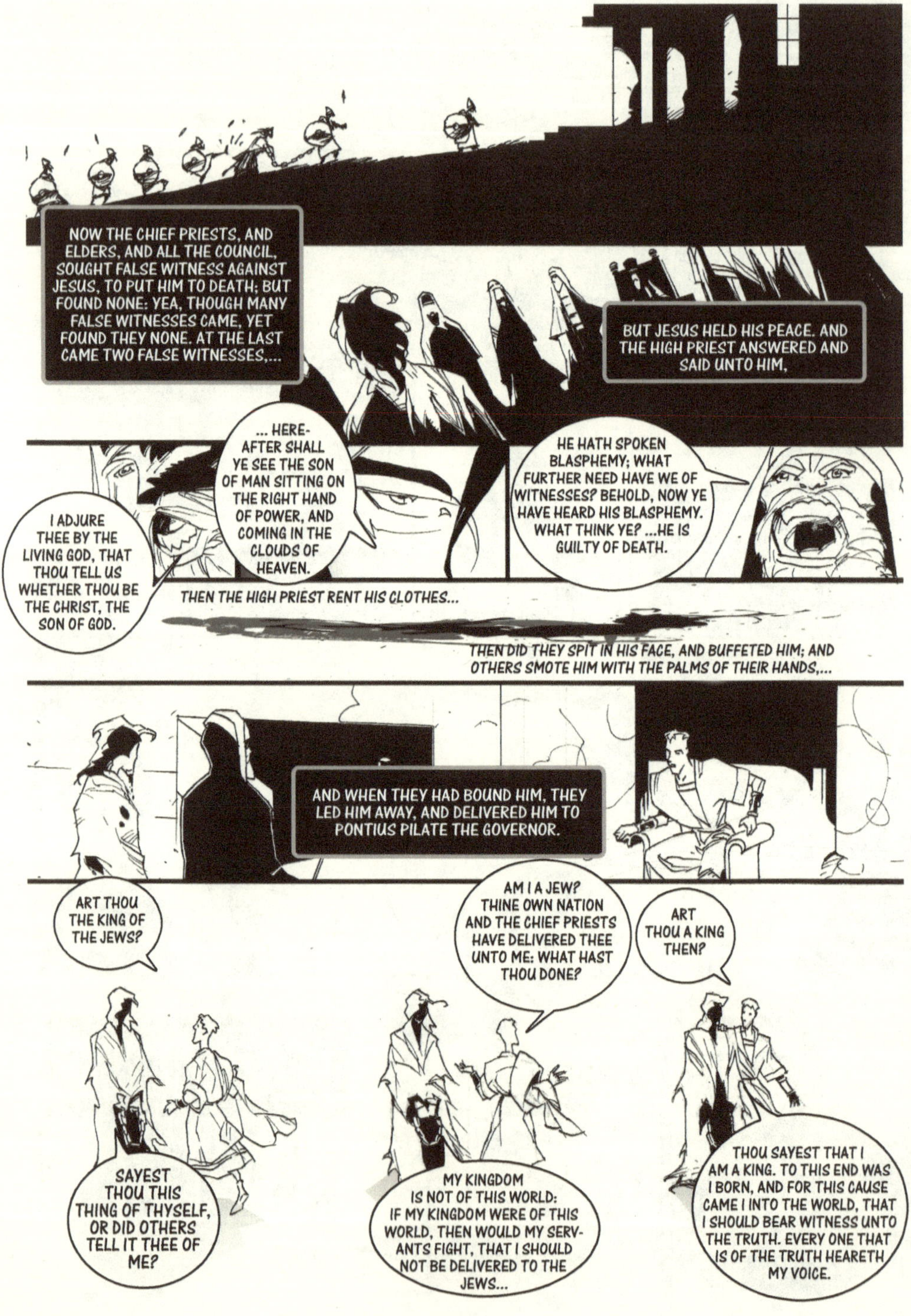

NOW THE CHIEF PRIESTS, AND ELDERS, AND ALL THE COUNCIL, SOUGHT FALSE WITNESS AGAINST JESUS, TO PUT HIM TO DEATH; BUT FOUND NONE: YEA, THOUGH MANY FALSE WITNESSES CAME, YET FOUND THEY NONE. AT THE LAST CAME TWO FALSE WITNESSES,...

BUT JESUS HELD HIS PEACE. AND THE HIGH PRIEST ANSWERED AND SAID UNTO HIM,

I ADJURE THEE BY THE LIVING GOD, THAT THOU TELL US WHETHER THOU BE THE CHRIST, THE SON OF GOD.

... HERE-AFTER SHALL YE SEE THE SON OF MAN SITTING ON THE RIGHT HAND OF POWER, AND COMING IN THE CLOUDS OF HEAVEN.

HE HATH SPOKEN BLASPHEMY; WHAT FURTHER NEED HAVE WE OF WITNESSES? BEHOLD, NOW YE HAVE HEARD HIS BLASPHEMY. WHAT THINK YE? ...HE IS GUILTY OF DEATH.

THEN THE HIGH PRIEST RENT HIS CLOTHES...

THEN DID THEY SPIT IN HIS FACE, AND BUFFETED HIM; AND OTHERS SMOTE HIM WITH THE PALMS OF THEIR HANDS,...

AND WHEN THEY HAD BOUND HIM, THEY LED HIM AWAY, AND DELIVERED HIM TO PONTIUS PILATE THE GOVERNOR.

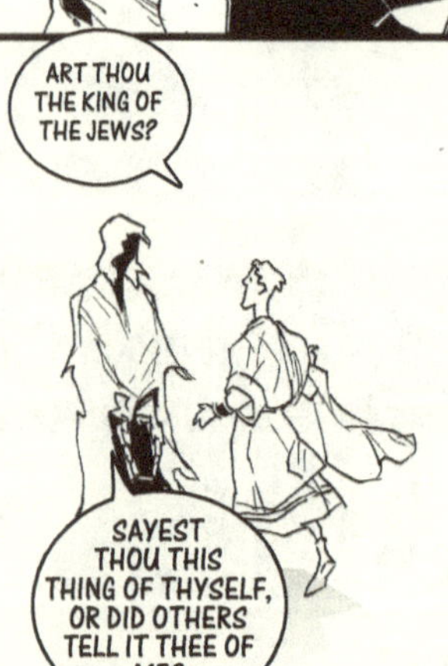

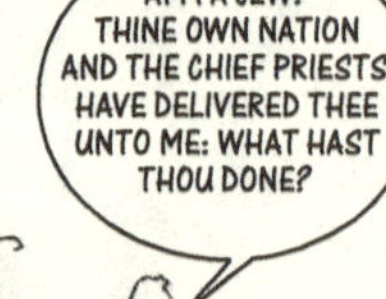

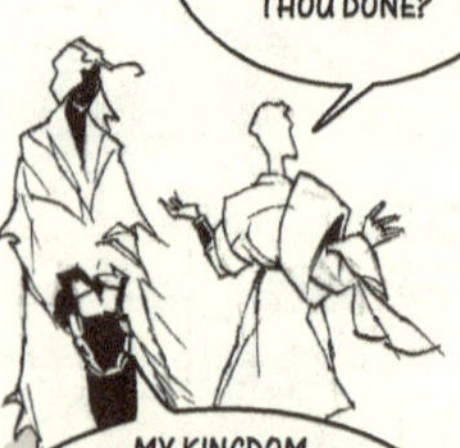

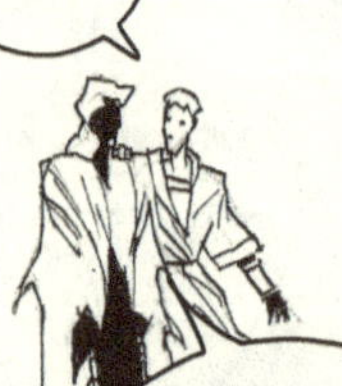

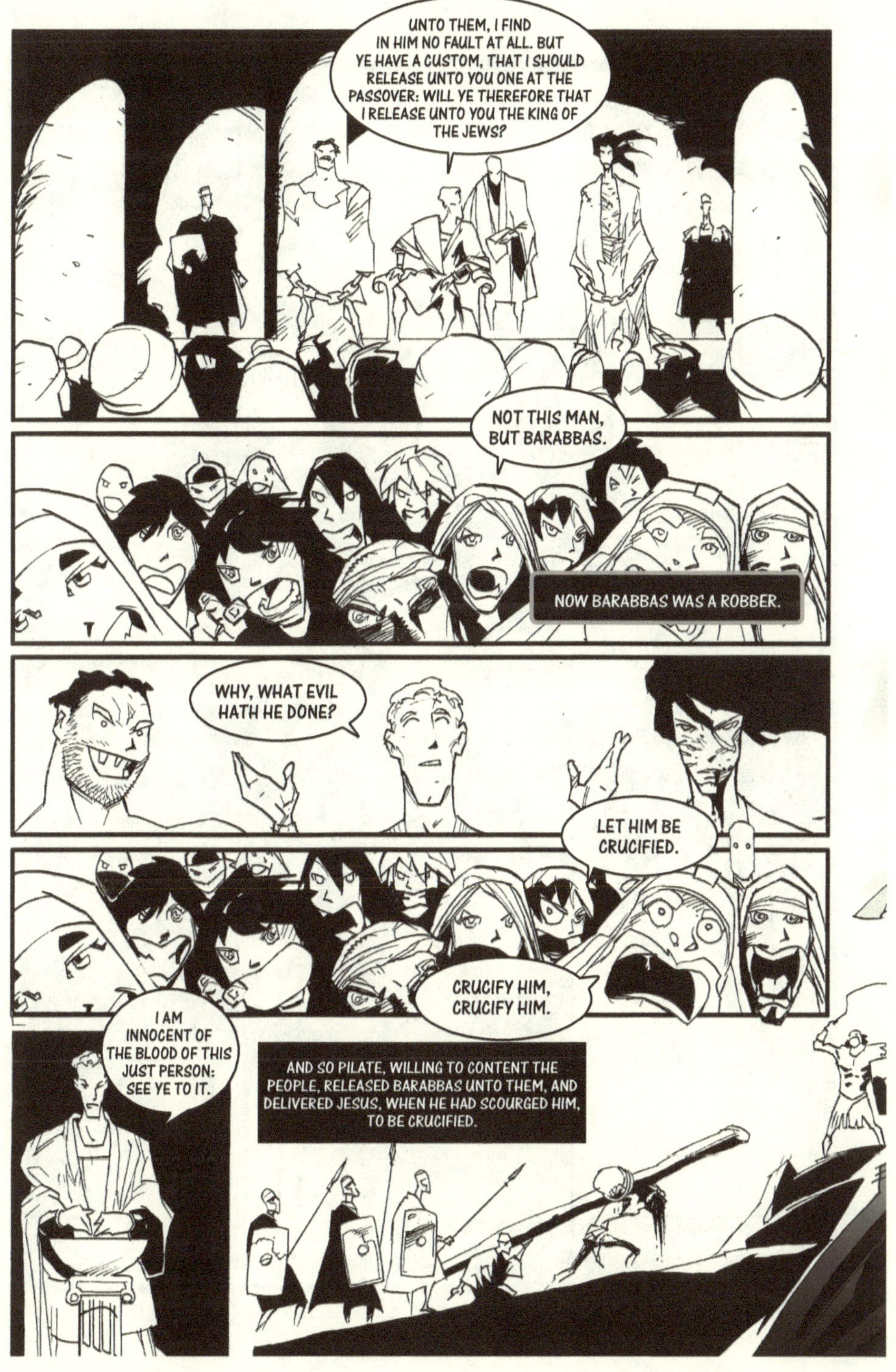
UNTO THEM, I FIND IN HIM NO FAULT AT ALL. BUT YE HAVE A CUSTOM, THAT I SHOULD RELEASE UNTO YOU ONE AT THE PASSOVER: WILL YE THEREFORE THAT I RELEASE UNTO YOU THE KING OF THE JEWS?
NOT THIS MAN, BUT BARABBAS.
NOW BARABBAS WAS A ROBBER.
WHY, WHAT EVIL HATH HE DONE?
LET HIM BE CRUCIFIED.
CRUCIFY HIM, CRUCIFY HIM.
I AM INNOCENT OF THE BLOOD OF THIS JUST PERSON: SEE YE TO IT.
AND SO PILATE, WILLING TO CONTENT THE PEOPLE, RELEASED BARABBAS UNTO THEM, AND DELIVERED JESUS, WHEN HE HAD SCOURGED HIM, TO BE CRUCIFIED.

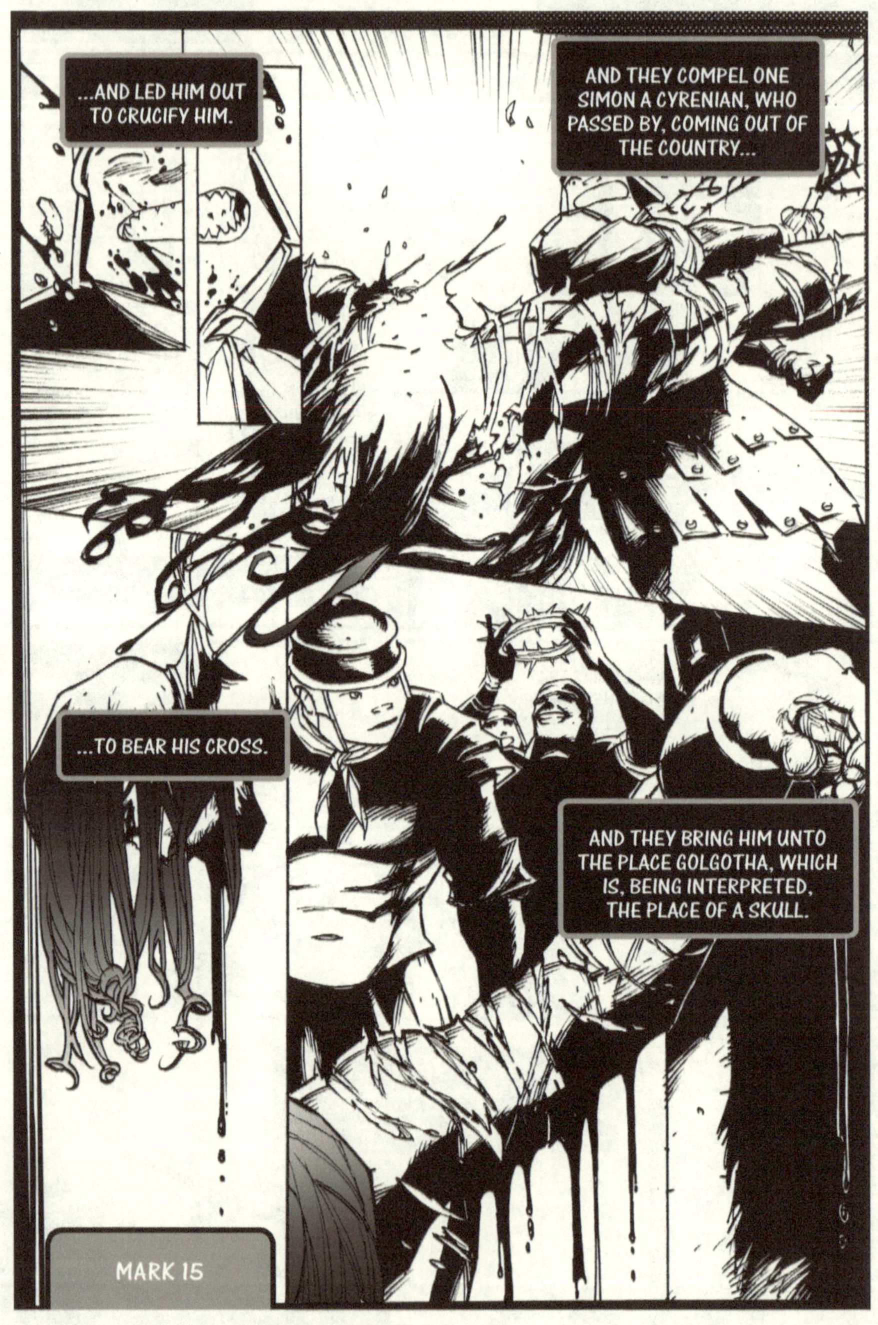
...AND LED HIM OUT TO CRUCIFY HIM.
AND THEY COMPEL ONE SIMON A CYRENIAN, WHO PASSED BY, COMING OUT OF THE COUNTRY...
...TO BEAR HIS CROSS.
AND THEY BRING HIM UNTO THE PLACE GOLGOTHA, WHICH IS, BEING INTERPRETED, THE PLACE OF A SKULL.
MARK 15

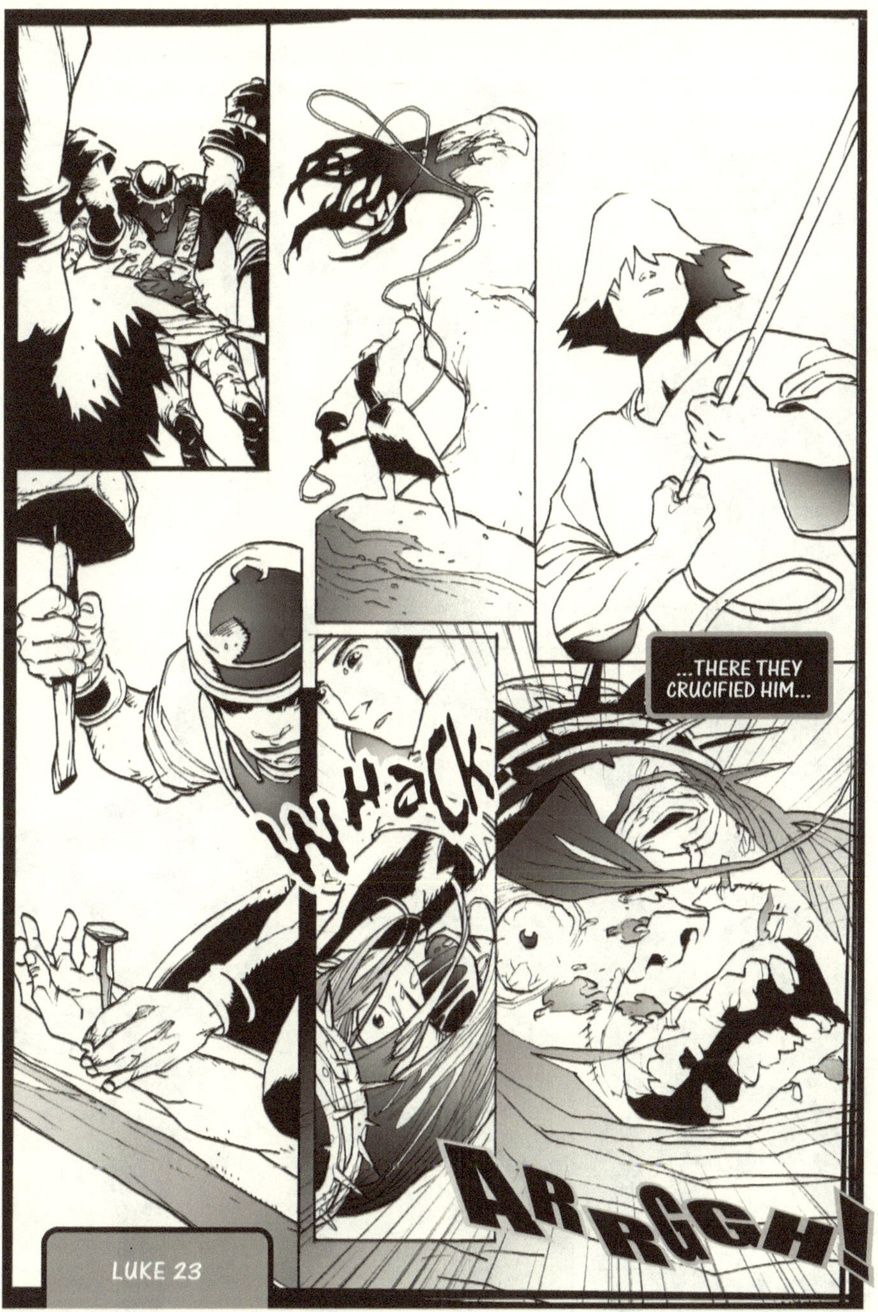
...THERE THEY CRUCIFIED HIM...
WHACK
ARRGGH!
LUKE 23

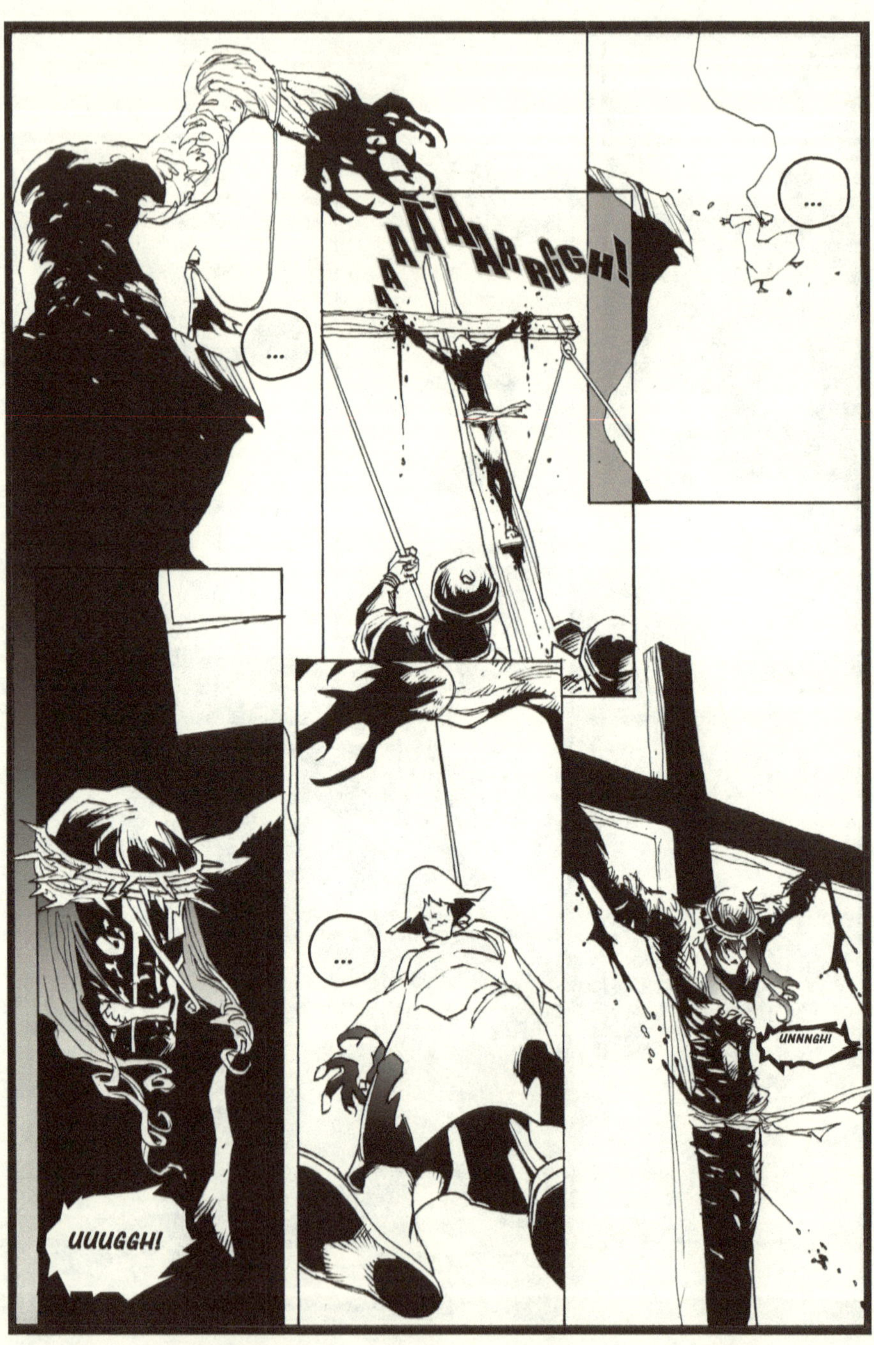
...
AAAAAARRGGH!
...
UUUGGH!
...
UNNNGH!

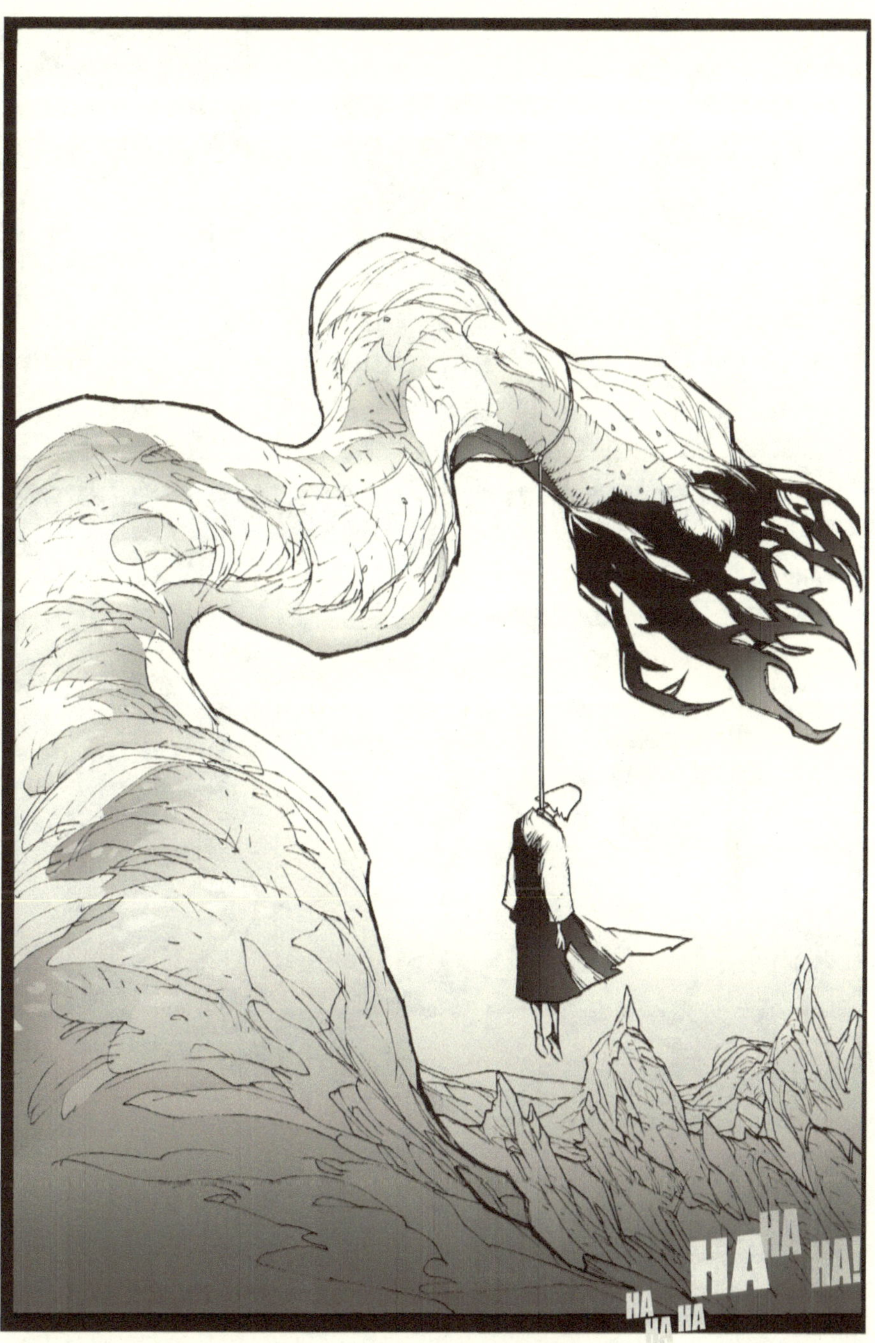
HA HA HA HA HA HA!

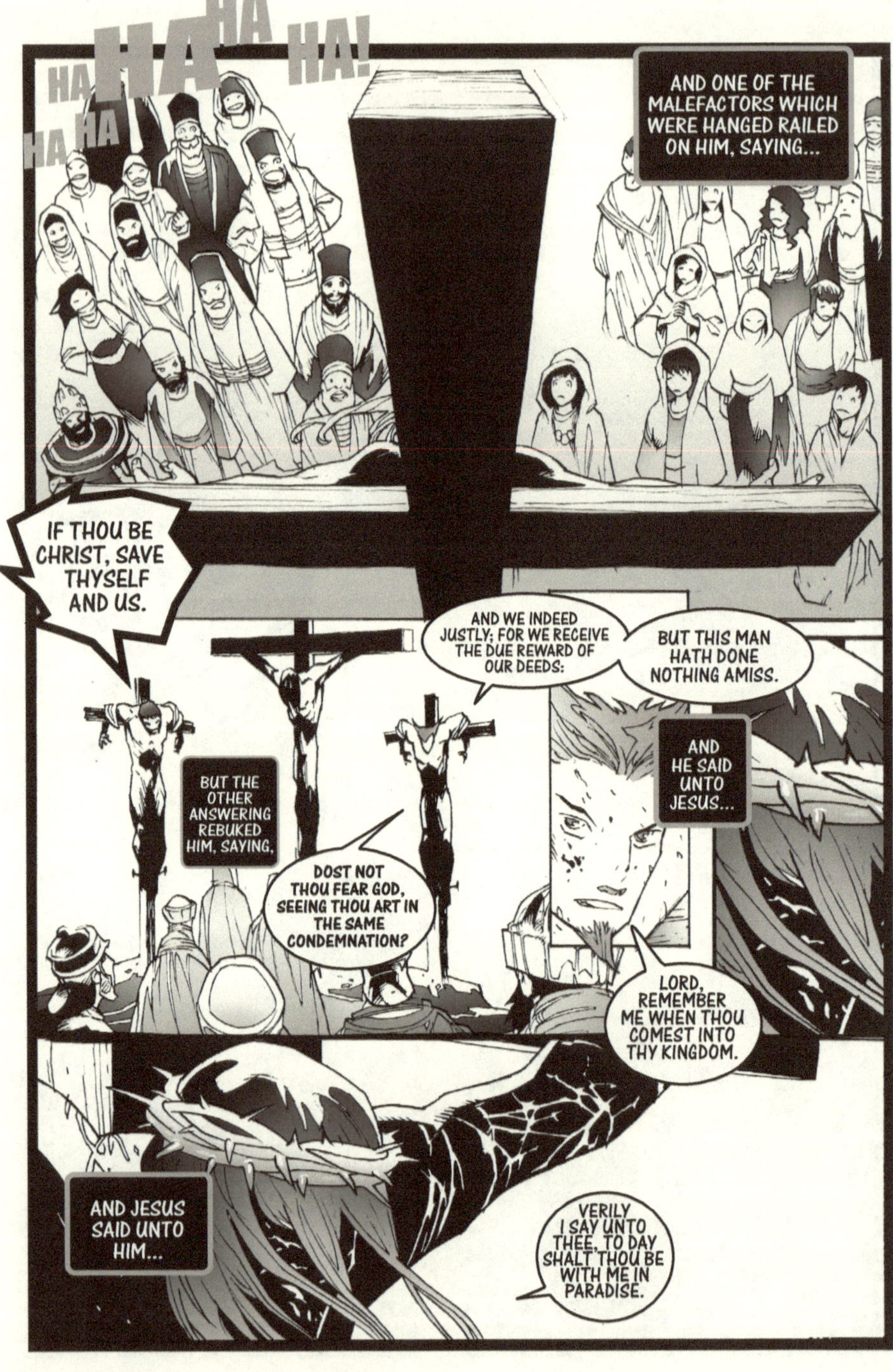
HA HA HA HA HA HA!
AND ONE OF THE MALEFACTORS WHICH WERE HANGED RAILED ON HIM, SAYING...
IF THOU BE CHRIST, SAVE THYSELF AND US.
BUT THE OTHER ANSWERING REBUKED HIM, SAYING,
DOST NOT THOU FEAR GOD, SEEING THOU ART IN THE SAME CONDEMNATION?
AND WE INDEED JUSTLY; FOR WE RECEIVE THE DUE REWARD OF OUR DEEDS:
BUT THIS MAN HATH DONE NOTHING AMISS.
AND HE SAID UNTO JESUS...
LORD, REMEMBER ME WHEN THOU COMEST INTO THY KINGDOM.
AND JESUS SAID UNTO HIM...
VERILY I SAY UNTO THEE, TO DAY SHALT THOU BE WITH ME IN PARADISE.

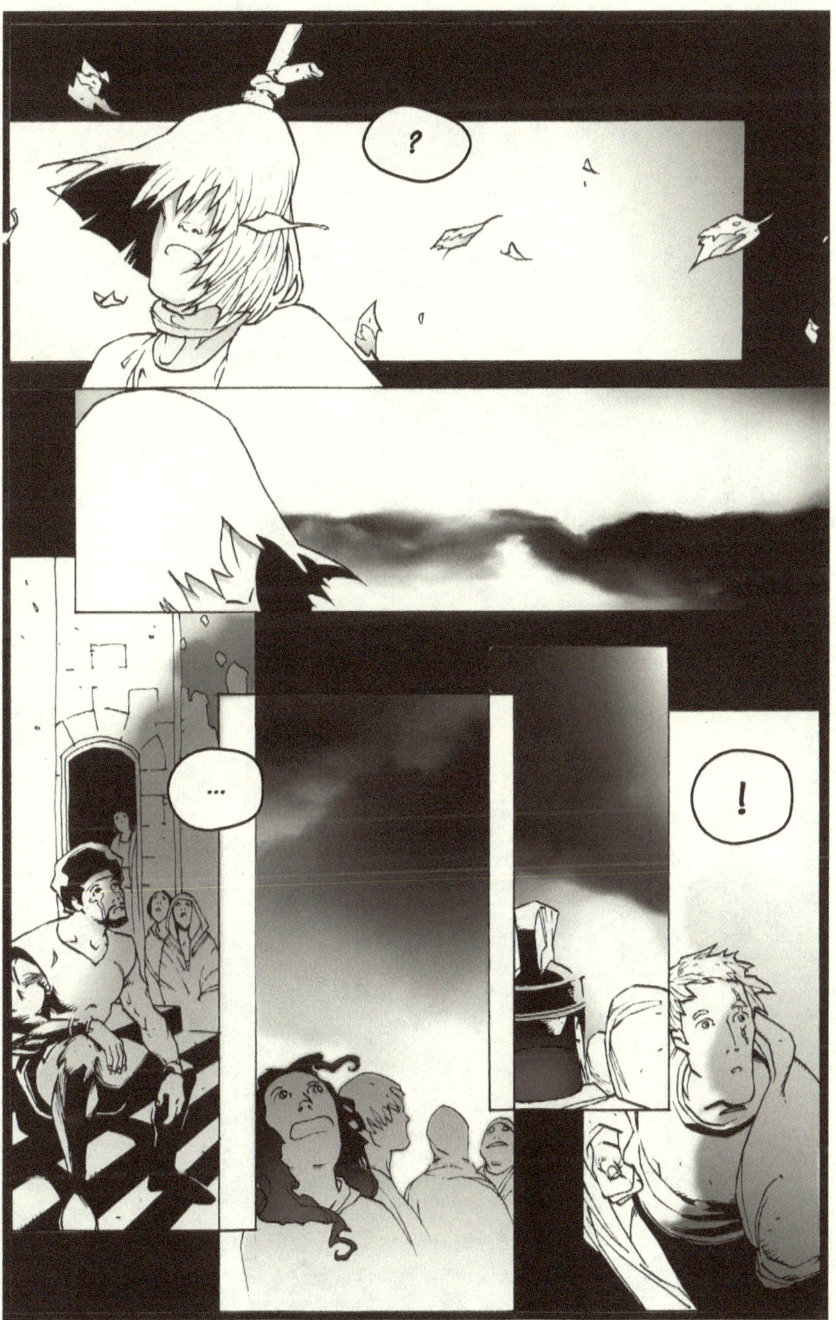

AND IT WAS ABOUT
THE SIXTH HOUR...

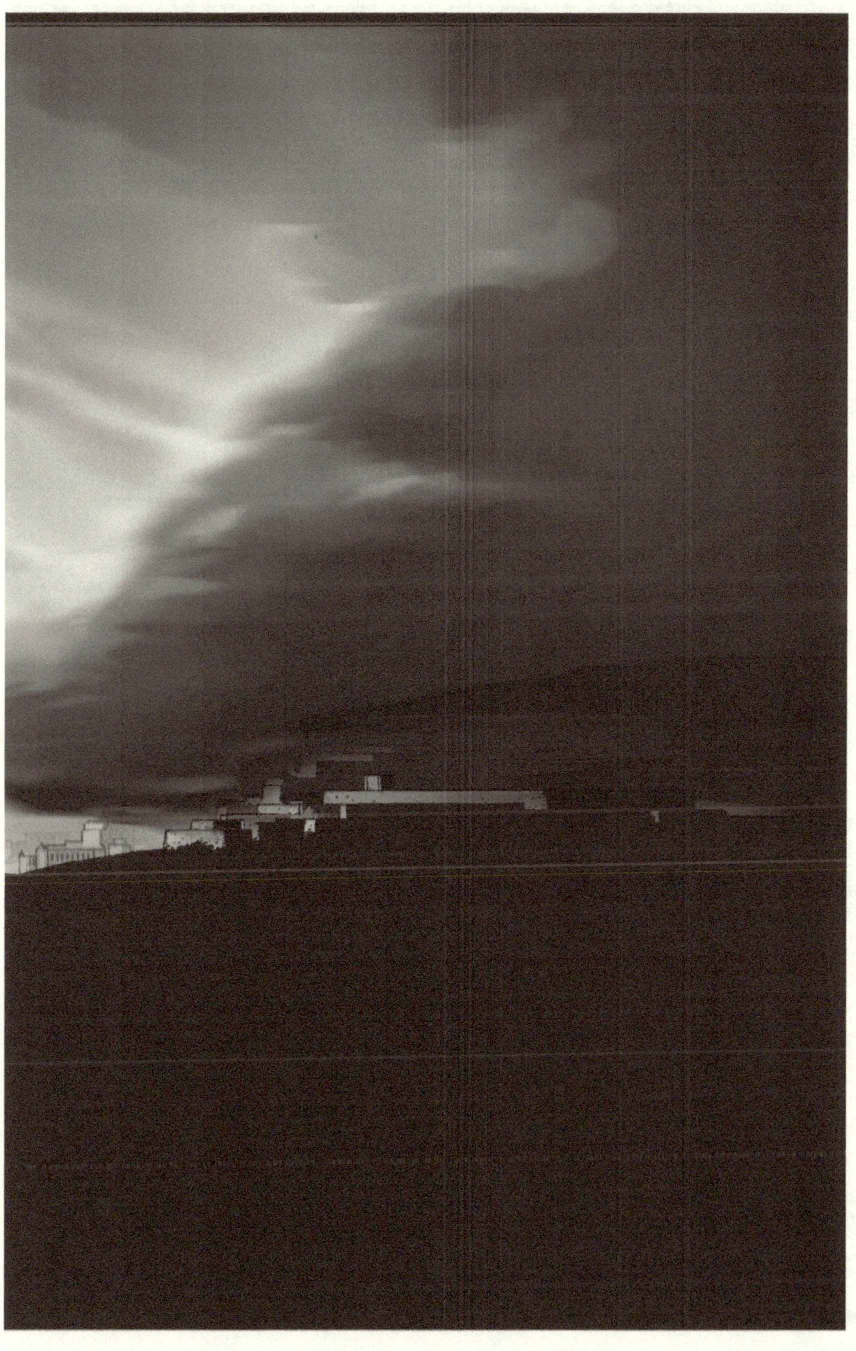

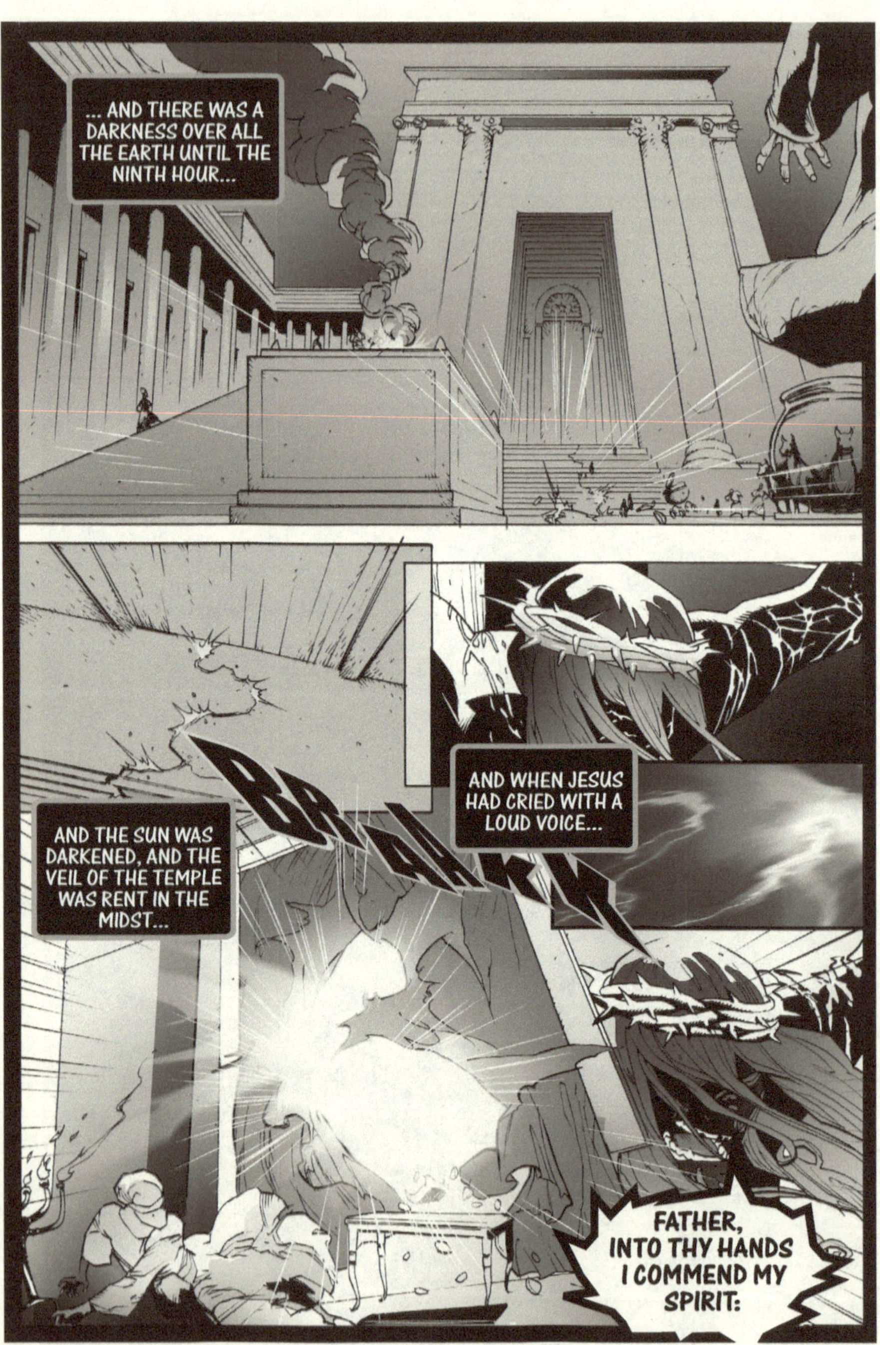
... AND THERE WAS A DARKNESS OVER ALL THE EARTH UNTIL THE NINTH HOUR...
AND THE SUN WAS DARKENED, AND THE VEIL OF THE TEMPLE WAS RENT IN THE MIDST...
AND WHEN JESUS HAD CRIED WITH A LOUD VOICE...
FATHER, INTO THY HANDS I COMMEND MY SPIRIT:

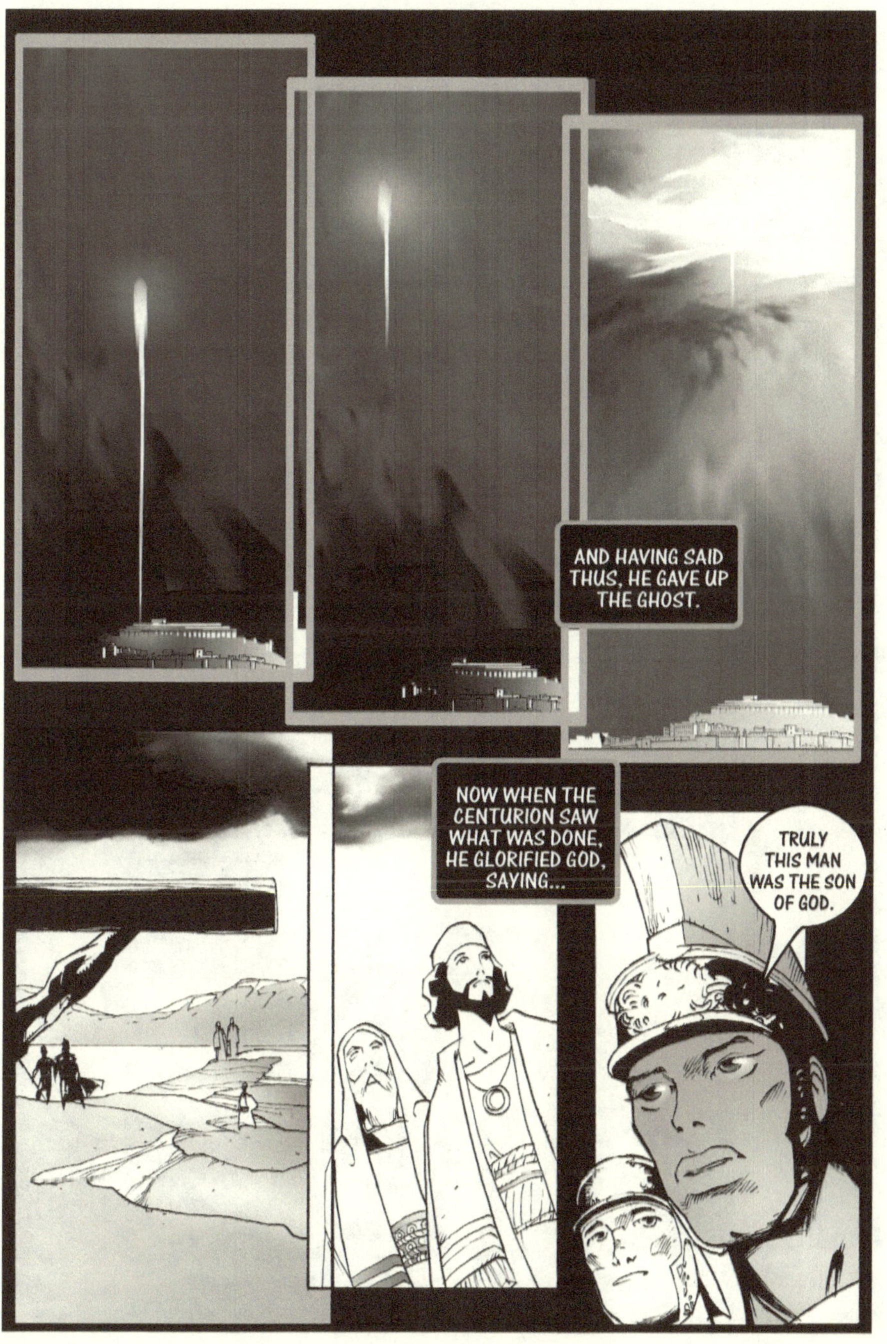
AND HAVING SAID THUS, HE GAVE UP THE GHOST.
NOW WHEN THE CENTURION SAW WHAT WAS DONE, HE GLORIFIED GOD, SAYING...
TRULY THIS MAN WAS THE SON OF GOD.

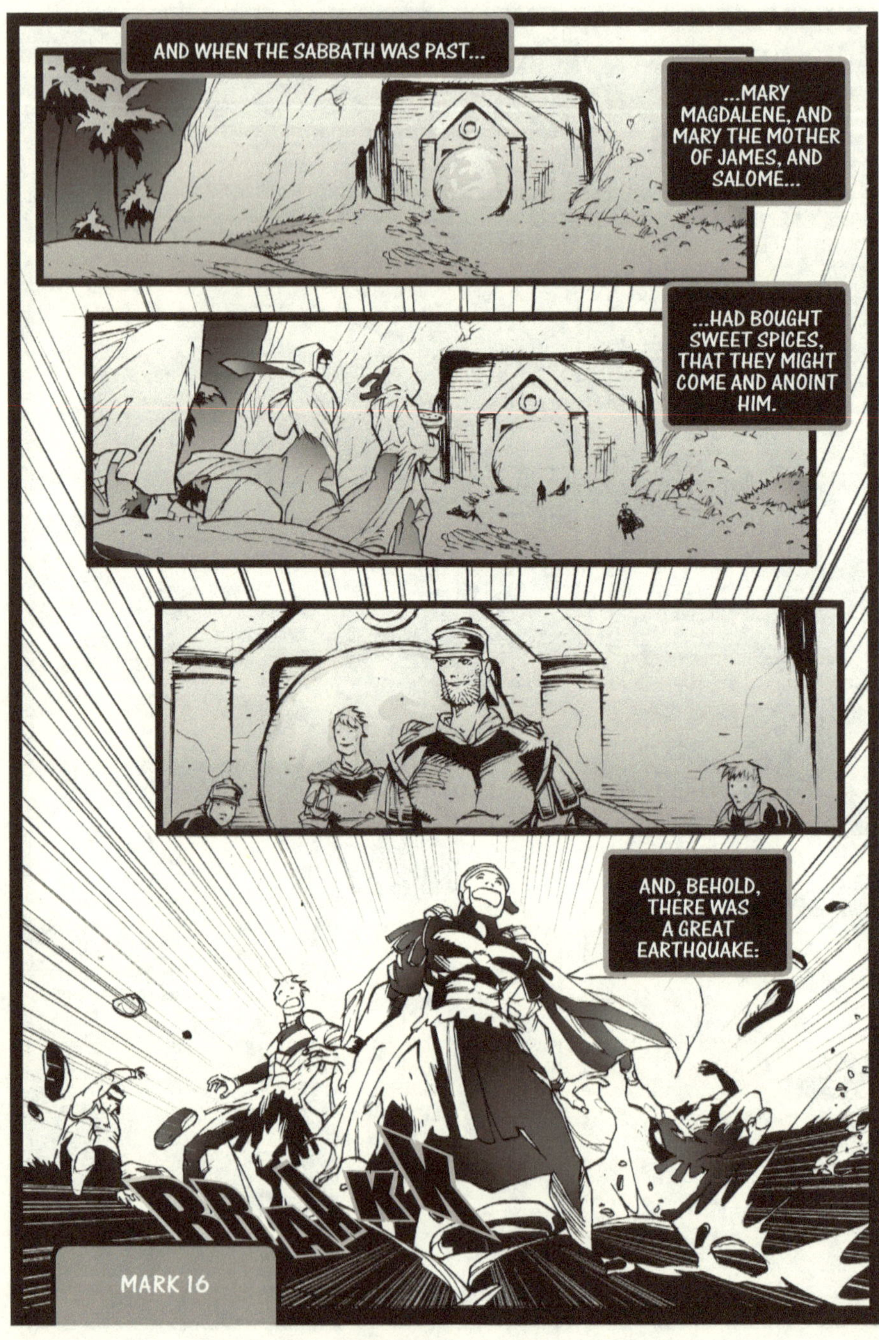
AND WHEN THE SABBATH WAS PAST...
...MARY MAGDALENE, AND MARY THE MOTHER OF JAMES, AND SALOME...
...HAD BOUGHT SWEET SPICES, THAT THEY MIGHT COME AND ANOINT HIM.
AND, BEHOLD, THERE WAS A GREAT EARTHQUAKE:
BRAKKA
MARK 16

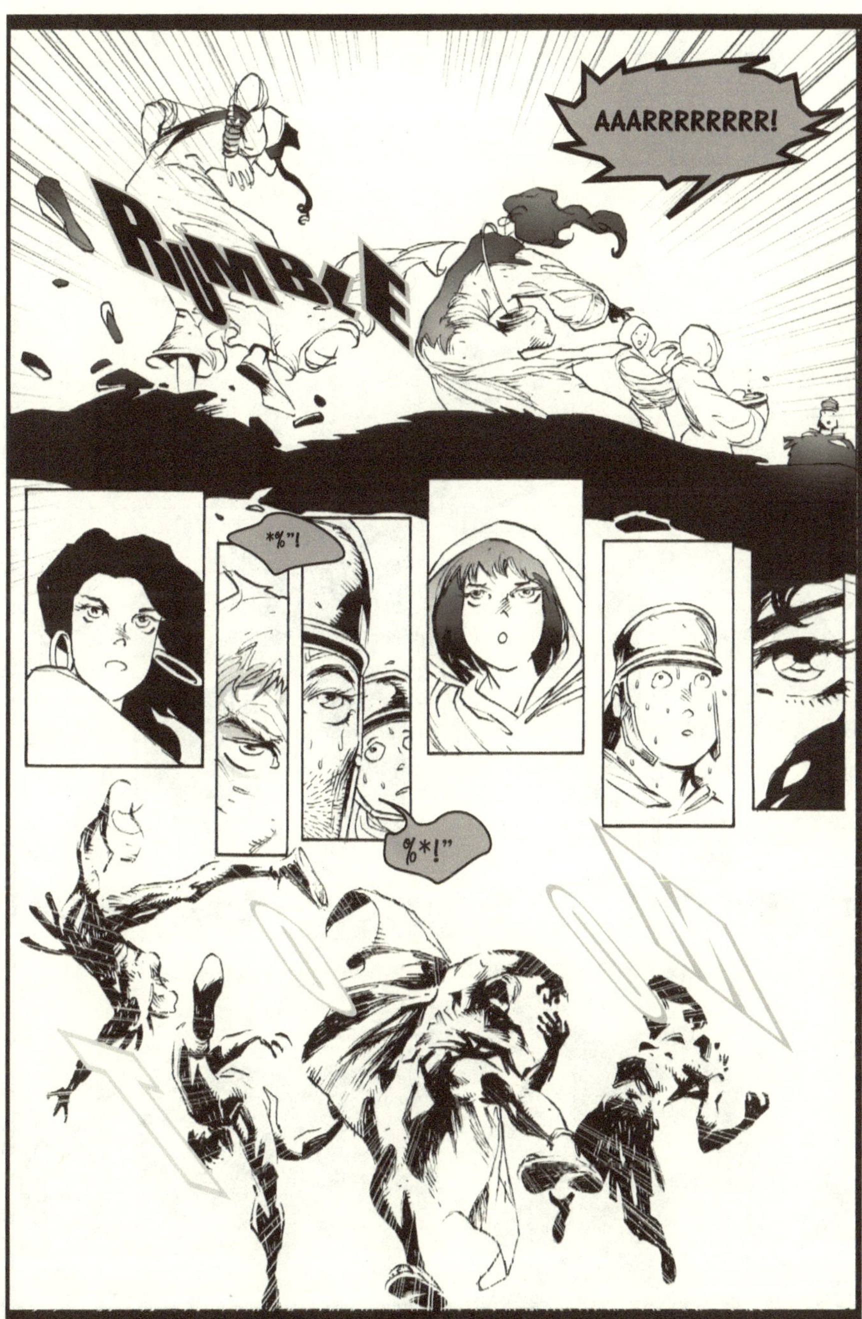

AAARRRRRRRR!
RUMBLE
*%"!
%*!"

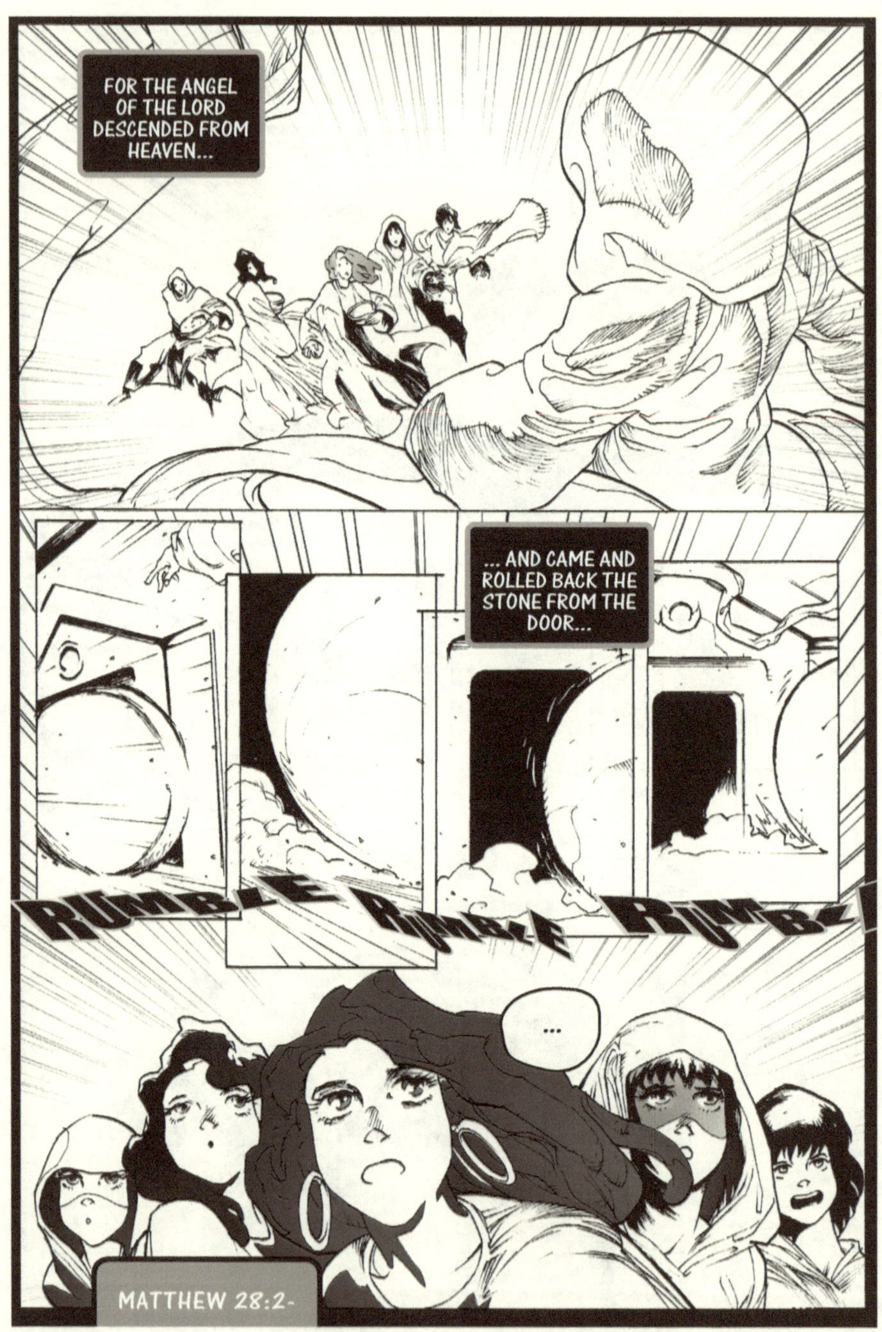
FOR THE ANGEL OF THE LORD DESCENDED FROM HEAVEN...
... AND CAME AND ROLLED BACK THE STONE FROM THE DOOR...
RUMBLE
RUMBLE
RUMBLE
...
MATTHEW 28:2-

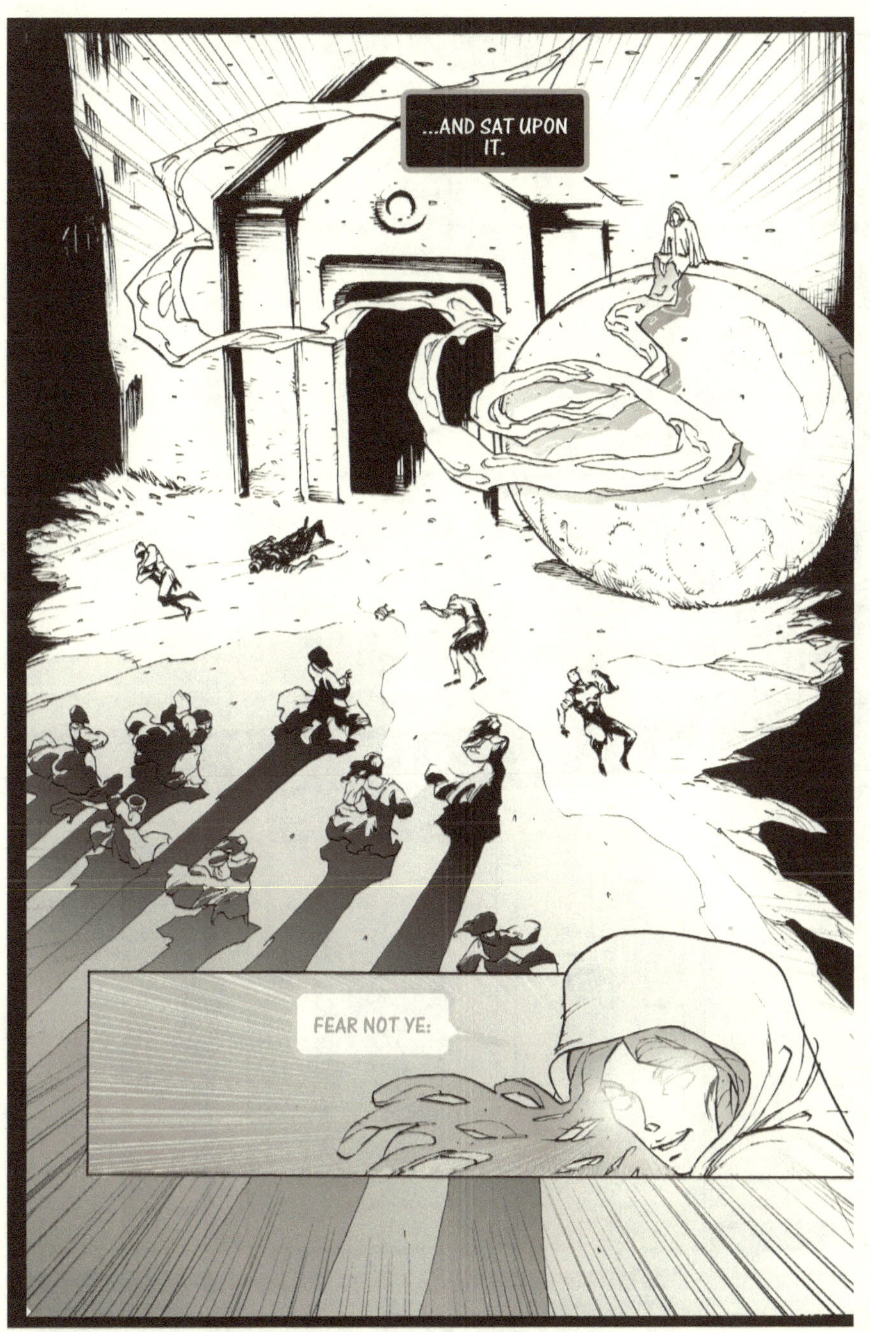
...AND SAT UPON IT.
FEAR NOT YE:

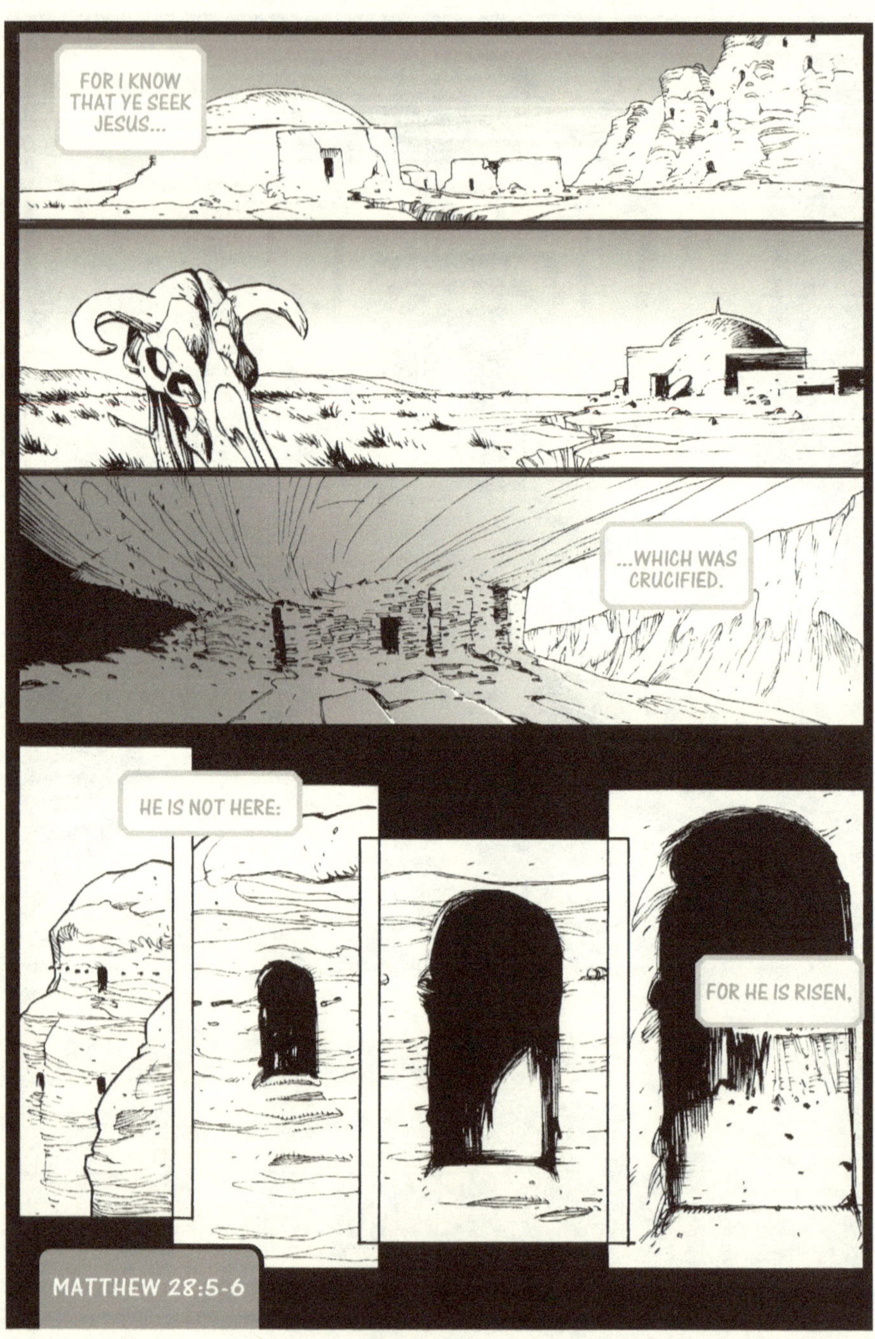
FOR I KNOW THAT YE SEEK JESUS...
...WHICH WAS CRUCIFIED.
HE IS NOT HERE:
FOR HE IS RISEN,
MATTHEW 28:5-6

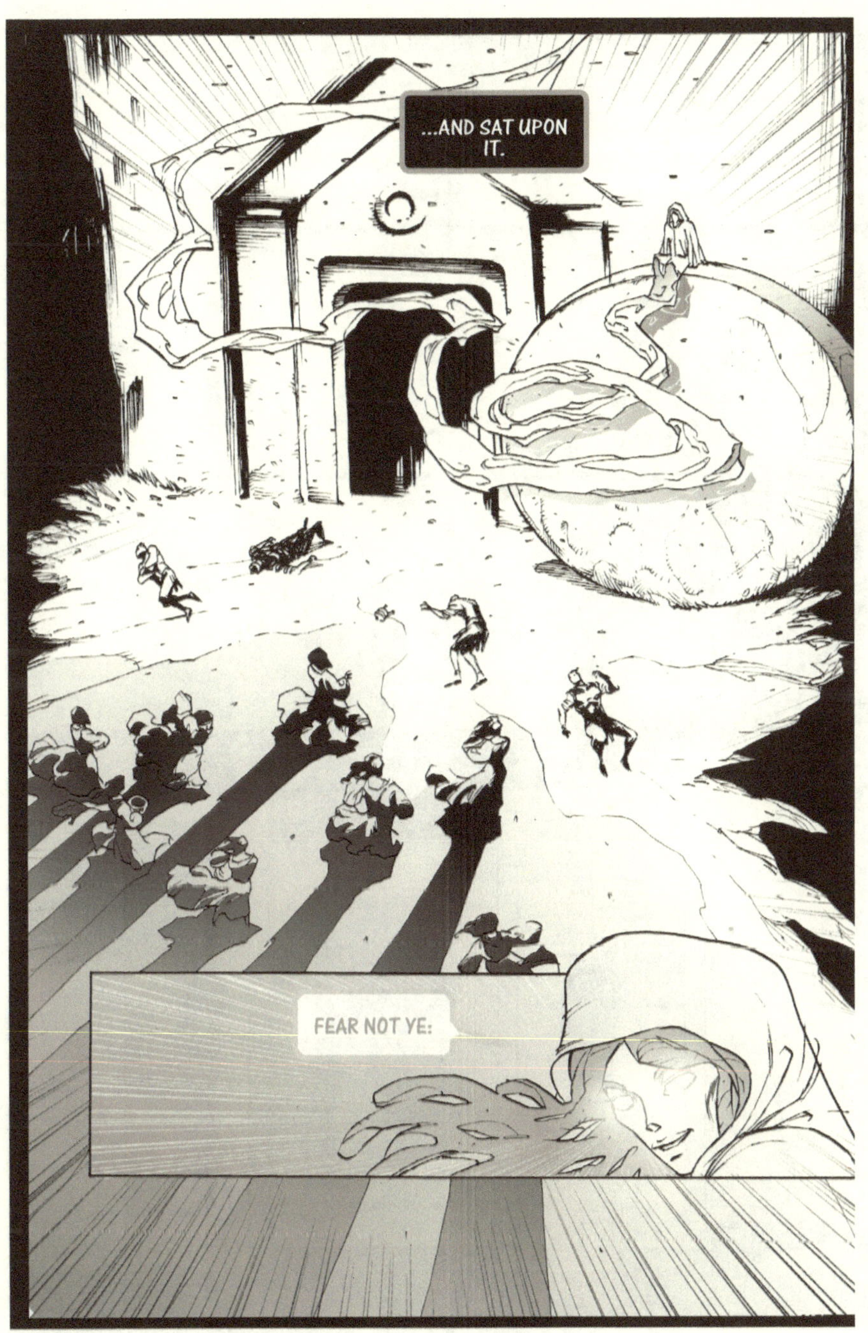
...AND SAT UPON IT.
FEAR NOT YE:

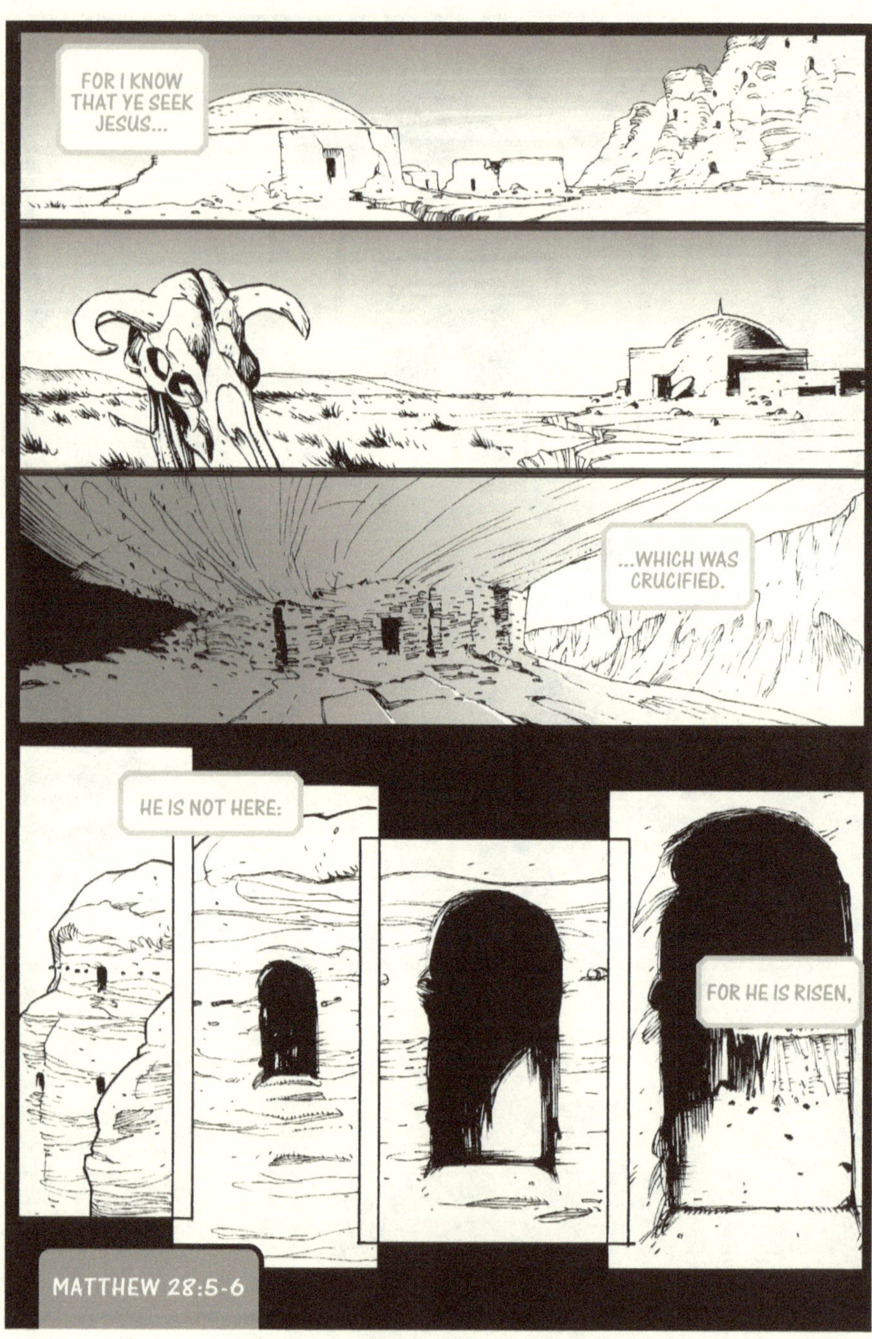
FOR I KNOW THAT YE SEEK JESUS...
...WHICH WAS CRUCIFIED.
HE IS NOT HERE:
FOR HE IS RISEN,
MATTHEW 28:5-6

THE ROMAN ROAD TO SALVATION

selected from Book of Romans King James version

The ROMANS ROAD....Romans were famous for their roads. This is a pathway you can walk that will lead you into a new life an eternal life.) These verses distil the path to Saving your soul.

Romans 3:10 As it is written: "There is none righteous, no, not one;" This means that there is no one who does right all of the time, or who is totally pure in heart and life.

Romans 3:23 "For all have sinned, and come short of the glory of God." No matter how good we live, there is still sin, missing the mark or point. We make errors, mess up in our lives. And, because of sin, we all fall short of what God wants us to be. We were born under the power of sin's control.

Romans 3:11 "There is none that understandeth; There is none that seeketh after God."
No one, left to oneself, will seek to find God, for one doesn't understand the condition one is in.

Romans 6:23a "For the wages of sin is death..."
"Wages" is payment or a paycheck. because we are sinners, if we die in our sins, the paycheck we wlll receive will be "death," eternal separation from God
Sin has an ending. It results in death. We all face physical death, which is a result of sin. But a worse death is spiritual death that alienates us from God, and will last for all eternity.

Romans 6:23b "...but the gift of God is eternal life through Jesus Christ our Lord."
Although we have a sin condition God offers a way of forgiveness of your sins and slavation ? Do you want to be saved? Salvation is a free gift from God to you! You can't earn this gift, but you must reach out and receive it by faith alone.
- Ask God to forgive you and save you.

Romans 5:8, "But God commendeth his love toward us, in that, while we were yet sinners, Christ died for us."

God loves you? Look at the cross. Christ was punished by death for your sins. Jesus died on the cross He paid sin's penalty. He paid the price for all sin, and when He took all the sins of the world on Himself on the cross, He bought us out of slavery to sin and death! The only condition is that we believe in Him and what He has done for us, understanding that we are now joined with Him, and that He is our life. He did all this because He loved us and gave Himself for us! His love is what saves you -- not religion,good works, lifestyle or church membership. God loves you!

Romans 10:13 "For whosoever shall call upon the name of the Lord shall be saved."

- Call out to God in the name of Jesus!

Romans 10:9,10 "That if thou shalt confess with thy mouth the Lord Jesus, and shalt believe in thine heart that God hath raised him from the dead, thou shalt be saved. For with the heart man believeth unto righteousness; and with the mouth confession is made unto salvation."

"Confess" **means to tell God what you believe about Jesus Christ. He wants to know that you believe Jesus is Lord and Savior, and that you believe His death on the cross was full payment for your sins past, present and the future. Next... 10:9b ...**and shalt believe in thine heart that God hath raised Him from the dead, **God wants to know that you believe that Jesus is alive today. Then...10:9c ...**thou shalt be saved. **That's God's promise: If you acknowledge your belief in Jesus' death, burial, and resurrection - that He did this for you - God will give you eternal life. How do you acknowledge this? Read one more verse.**

10:10 For with the heart man believeth unto righteousness; and with the mouth confession is made unto salvation.

- If you know that God is knocking on your heart's door, ask Him to come into your heart.

Seize the Opportunity!!!!

Revelation 3:20a "Behold, I stand at the door, and knock: if any man hear my voice, and open the door, I will come in to him, and will sup with him, and he with me."

Believe in Him. Ask Him to come in to your heart by faith, and ask Him to reveal Himself to you

www.ingramcontent.com/pod-product-compliance
Lightning Source LLC
La Vergne TN
LVHW050939080826
845145LV00004B/1326

* 9 7 8 0 9 5 6 9 7 3 1 1 5 *